The deeply rich and nuanced skill set req[uir]ing to children with trauma has too often [...] now, Karyn Purvis and Lisa Qualls provide a wealth of research-based expertise and personal experience that will change the life of any adult caring for a child who knows "hard places." They offer a wide variety of practical tools for understanding the core (and often hidden) needs of children struggling with trauma. Their compassionate, wise, and clinically proven step-by-step options can alter the outcome of any child's life. My deep gratitude to Karyn Purvis and Lisa Qualls for making this practical and life-altering option available in such a clear, accessible, and compassionate way.

Kent Hoffman
cofounder of Circle of Security and coauthor of *Raising a Secure Child*

When caring for children from hard places, feelings of love are simply not enough. This book addresses so many topics close to our own hearts and personal story. The real-life accounts of walking through the hardest places will bring the hope and healing that are so desperately needed. To Karyn Purvis and Lisa Qualls, thank you for an amazing resource that everyone in the adoption community can use on their own path toward restoration.

Mary Beth Chapman
cofounder of Show Hope

Providing care for children who come from "hard places" isn't easy. These children think and act with few assumptions of safety and trust. To connect with these children, we need to understand and attend to their underlying fear and shame while ensuring that we are approachable and trustworthy ourselves. Karyn and Lisa remind us again and again about the power of relationships in promoting healing and development, and they provide many practical strategies to assist us in our journey. They also remind us of the need to begin at the beginning, creating safety and connection, balancing nurture with predictability and structure, while modeling the attitude and behaviors we hope to teach. *The Connected Parent* complements Karyn's earlier work, *The Connected Child*, and highlights the need for parents to understand and care for themselves while providing their children with the comfort and joy they desperately need. This journey may be hard, so you would do well to keep this book at your side.

Dan Hughes
author and founder of Dyadic Developmental Psychotherapy

When I met Dr. Karyn Purvis, I was immediately in awe of her gentle spirit and her wisdom. Her book *The Connected Child* is the most ragged, worn-out book in my house because I referred to it over and over in moments of desperation in parenting children from hard places. *The Connected Parent* will soon look the same, as it is full of wisdom and insight that I will refer to continually. This book is for all parents who long to love their children with compassion and tenderness. I'm so thankful that the work of Dr. Purvis lives on at the Karyn Purvis Institute of Child Development at Texas Christian University and through Lisa Qualls and this book!

Katie Davis Majors
author of *Kisses from Katie* and *Daring to Hope*
founder of Amazima Ministries

Lisa Qualls has done a masterful job of weaving her family's story together with the powerful legacy of the late Dr. Karyn Purvis. A must-read for parents who long to attach successfully to their adopted kids.

Sherrie Eldridge
author of *Twenty Things Adopted Kids Wish Their Adoptive Parents Knew*

Tragically, many traumatized children are greatly misunderstood. Dr. Karyn Purvis knew how to reach these children and begin the process of healing. In her final written work, *The Connected Parent*, Dr. Purvis shares her wisdom and expertise for working with children who have experienced trauma. She had a heart as big as Texas, and we are so thrilled that her work continues to help vulnerable children and families all around the world.

Deborra-lee Jackman
adoptive parent and founder of Adopt Change and Hopeland

This is the book foster and adoptive parents have waited for. Dr. Karyn Purvis taught so many of us about our children and how to play a part in their healing. Receiving more insight and instruction from Dr. Purvis posthumously is an unexpected gift, and it is made complete by the compassionate wisdom and experience of fellow foster and adoptive mother Lisa Qualls. Together, their voices create a more complete roadmap for foster and adoptive parents as they love and parent children from hard places.

Jamie Finn
speaker and author of *Foster the Family*

This gem of a book provides parents with a holistic, research-based parenting approach for children who have endured trauma. Karyn Purvis's clear voice provides the science behind children's struggles and effective parenting approaches. Lisa brings the book home with her scripts, examples, and tips on behavioral interventions. The authors connect aptly with their readers even as they help us to connect with children. This compassionate book touched my heart. I am grateful to Karyn Purvis for her legacy through this book, made the richer through joint authorship by Lisa Qualls.

Deborah Gray
author of *Promoting Healthy Attachments*; *Attaching with Love, Hugs, and Play*;
Nurturing Adoptions; and *Attaching in Adoption*

This amazing book continues the legacy of Dr. Karyn Purvis and her ground-breaking techniques in helping children and families do the work of healing. Joining with Dr. Purvis, Lisa Qualls brilliantly weaves real-life challenges and methods through every chapter, offering hope and practical, realistic strategies. This book will make a great resource for foster and adoptive parent book clubs and support groups. I recommend it highly!

Jayne Schooler
author of *Wound Children, Healing Homes*;
Telling the Truth to Your Adopted or Foster Child, and
The Whole Life Adoption Book

What a gift this book is to anyone working and living with children from hard places. How many of us have longed for someone whispering in our ear, telling us how to apply Dr. Purvis's principles in the heat of the moment? Lisa Qualls shares vulnerably about her family in a relatable way, allowing us to learn and be inspired to grow alongside of her. This way of parenting is a game changer, and over the long haul, it brings the peace we long for in our challenging stories.

Beth Guckenberger
author, missionary, and adoptive and foster parent

In *The Connected Parent*, the truth of psychology and clinical research is paired with the grace of real-life-in-the-trenches parenting in such a way that all who read it will feel better equipped to care for children from "hard places"—and empowered to reject the whispers of shame and failure they will inevitably confront along the journey. This is a must-have book.

Jason Johnson
speaker and author of *Reframing Foster Care*

Dr. Karyn Purvis and Lisa Qualls have written a must-read for adults who want to understand how to serve and love children as well as themselves. This book gives adults permission to embark on a journey of self-discovery as they usher children through their own journey. Such a practical and sophisticated book...a gift of love to the world.

Daren Jones
Karyn Purvis Institute of Child Development

The Connected Child was a life changer for my family—what a gift that we now get the incredible continuation of Dr. Purvis's work in *The Connected Parent*. Her rich knowledge of attachment, sensory processing, and neuroscience as they relate to relational trauma are brought to life with Lisa Qualls's abundant and heart-filled stories. Written with compassion and empathy, *The Connected Parent* will serve as a necessary resource for adoptive and foster families for generations to come!

Jessica Honegger
founder of Noonday Collection, author of *Imperfect Courage*

The
Connected
Parent

The
Connected
Parent

KARYN PURVIS, PhD.
& LISA QUALLS

WITH EMMELIE PICKETT

HARVEST HOUSE PUBLISHERS
EUGENE, OREGON

Cover design by Studio Gearbox

Cover photo © Amir Kaljikovic / Stocksy

TRUST-BASED RELATIONAL INTERVENTION and TBRI are federally registered trademarks of Texas Christian University.

This book includes stories in which people's names and some details of their situations have been changed.

The Connected Parent
Copyright © 2020 by Lisa Qualls
Published by Harvest House Publishers
Eugene, Oregon 97408
www.harvesthousepublishers.com

ISBN 978-0-7369-7892-7 (pbk.)
ISBN 978-0-7369-7893-4 (eBook)
ISBN 978-0-7369-8299-3 (eAudio)

Library of Congress Cataloging-in-Publication Data

Names: Purvis, Karyn, author. | Qualls, Lisa, author.
Title: The connected parent / Dr. Karyn Purvis and Lisa Qualls ; with
    Emmelie Picket.
Description: Eugene : Harvest House Publishers, 2020.
Identifiers: LCCN 2019060259 (print) | LCCN 2019060260 (ebook) | ISBN
    9780736978927 (paperback) | ISBN 9780736978934 (ebook)
Subjects: LCSH: Parenting. | Parenting--Psychological aspects. | Parent and
    child.
Classification: LCC HQ755.8 .P87 2020 (print) | LCC HQ755.8 (ebook) | DDC
    306.874--dc23
LC record available at https://lccn.loc.gov/2019060259
LC ebook record available at https://lccn.loc.gov/2019060260

Printed in the United States of America

23 24 25 26 27 28 / BP-RD / 10 9 8

For Russ, my safe haven and deepest love. We could not have imagined the adventures we would have together.

For Hannah, Mary Kate, Noah, Samuel, Isaiah, Annarose, B.E., Kalkidan, Claire, Ebenezer, Wogayu, Bella, and Nick—you are my sweetest treasures.

Kalkidan—one day we'll eat spicy food together again in heaven. There will be no tears or sorrow, only love.

And to God, the author and perfecter of my faith—your plans are so much bigger than I ever dreamed. My heart and life are yours.

—LQ

For RP, who grounds me and challenges me. Your encouragement and love mean everything to me.

For Tate, who helps me look back and remember and look forward and hope. And for Navy, who helps me find joy right where I am.

And for Karyn, who taught me much from the stage, in the air, on the road, and across the table over the years and miles. You changed my life.

To the one from whom all these blessings flow, my God and Father. To you be the glory.

—EP

Contents

Part 1: The Heart of Relationships

Part 2: Real-Life Strategies

Part 3: Hope and Strength for the Journey

Foreword

by David R. Cross

This book is a celebration of the creative genius of the late Dr. Karyn Purvis. Dr. Purvis qualifies as a genius for two reasons. The first is that she synthesized a wide range of information and created something entirely new—that which we now call Trust-Based Relational Intervention (TBRI). Dr. Purvis synthesized information from the deep roots of her faith, from her scientific understanding of children's development, and from the rich web of her own caregiving experiences as parent, foster parent, and minister's wife. She blended all of this into a seamless whole that teaches us all how to be better parents and caregivers.

The second reason we can say that Dr. Purvis qualifies as a creative genius is that her creation (TBRI) possesses extraordinary value for everyone. It meets fundamental needs of all people, irrespective of faith, geography, or personal wealth. We live in a world that has lost its way when it comes to caregiving, and TBRI can help us find our way back. The demand for TBRI continues to grow as more and more parents and professionals learn TBRI and experience firsthand its transformational power. TBRI is spreading across the United States and the rest of the world, mostly by word of mouth.

In addition to being a celebration of the creative genius of Dr. Purvis, this book is a celebration of the authors' dedication to bringing it into being. It is especially a celebration of the story Lisa and Russ Qualls share, which makes this book special. Their story makes this book sing and brings life to the TBRI principles and strategies. Readers of this book will have the best of two worlds: On one hand, they will hear the voice of Dr. Purvis as she shares her wisdom about caring for children "from hard places." On the other, they will hear the voice of parents who have walked the walk and have struggled with implementing and mastering the TBRI principles and strategies. Readers should also know that this book would not have been completed without the help of Emmelie Pickett, who so capably stood in for Dr. Purvis and helped bring the book across the finish line.

Finally, this book is a celebration of the selfless dedication of all those parents, like Lisa and Russ, who bring children into their homes to raise as their own. I benefited from this kind of selfless dedication as a child, and I know firsthand the impact it can have. Indeed, I would not be writing these words today if not for those, like Lisa and Russ, who stepped into my life to care for me and launch me on my life journey. The journey Lisa and Russ have chosen as adoptive parents is not an easy one, which is why TBRI is so important. The dedication and love that adoptive and foster parents bring to the equation is not enough. That sense of mission and purpose must be matched by knowledge and strategies that empower parents to be successful. This book helps fill that void.

Introduction

Lisa

Russ and I had been married twenty-two years and had seven children by birth when our eyes were opened to the orphan crisis in Ethiopia. We were not perfect parents, but we were good parents who loved our children and had a deep faith. With kids ranging in age from four to twenty, our life was rich and full. We had something beautiful and wanted to share it with children who needed a family.

Our adoption journey began with a phone call on Valentine's Day 2006 as I was cleaning the kitchen after lunch. My friend Emily called with the exciting news that she and her husband, Mark, were adopting two little boys from Ethiopia. That call flung open an unexpected door, and we walked into the next chapter of our lives.

I remember telling Emily perhaps Russ and I should adopt. We had numerous conversations, and at one point she said, "While you're working on making that decision, you can always sponsor a child at AHOPE" (an orphanage for children living with HIV). I quickly contacted them and asked to sponsor a child. Soon an envelope arrived in the mail with a photo of a sad-looking little girl wearing a frilly dress, her head shaved and tears in her eyes. We put it on our refrigerator and thought of her daily.

It wasn't long before we began the process to adopt two little boys from Ethiopia. I was a single-minded woman, filling out paperwork, making calls, and running to and from our bank to have documents notarized. We bought a photocopier, and I developed a close relationship with our FedEx office. I could not stop until it was done.

Just before Thanksgiving, we got referrals for our two little boys. The older was nineteen months old, and the baby was only one month old.

And Then There Were Three...and Four

During this time, Emily and Mark traveled to Ethiopia to get their two little boys, and while in Addis Ababa, they visited AHOPE. There they met the little girl we were sponsoring. She was stunning and energetic and had the sweetest dimples they had ever seen.

The nurse told Emily, "We hope your friends will adopt her." Surprised, she answered, "They're not planning to adopt her—they're already adopting two little boys." We didn't know it was possible to adopt a child living with HIV. Besides, we were already adding two little boys to our family.

This little girl, however, did not leave my mind. I thought of her with no mother or father to comfort her when she was sick or to answer her cries when she was scared. I imagined her sleeping in a room filled with rows of bunk beds yet feeling very much alone.

In 2006, we also knew very little about HIV. Would she live? Would it be safe for our other children? We researched, talked, sought advice, and prayed. Soon another door was opened, and we walked through it. The little girl on our refrigerator was soon to become our daughter.

I began plowing through paperwork again and submitted the adoption forms for our daughter only a few months later.

At the time, the process of adopting from Ethiopia was very fast, and in February 2007 (one year from Emily's phone call), we traveled to Addis Ababa to meet our three children. Taking them in our arms, we smiled and cried with full hearts. It was an incredible day, seeing the longing of our hearts and the realization of efforts fulfilled.

We also met another little girl who touched our hearts. She was funny and sweet, and when we returned home, we found her in many of our photos from the trip. We thought of her often, and she grew in our hearts. We returned to Ethiopia, and she joined our family in August 2008.

Was Something Wrong?

We had read books, received training, and learned that it would take time for our children to trust us, accept us, attach to us, and begin healing. But we were experiencing extreme challenges. One of our children was so wounded that her suffering was impacting all of us.

We prayed, we talked, we cried. We wondered how it all could go so wrong and questioned whether it was our fault. Had we made a dreadful mistake? Had we brought this suffering upon our family? Other families seemed to be doing well...was something wrong with us? It was a dark and dreadful place to be. We felt shame over our apparently insufficient parenting skills and our inability to bring healing to our child.

Convinced that nobody could understand the chaos in our home, we withdrew into our private struggle. Many of our days were spent simply trying to keep everyone safe. It was not uncommon for Russ to come home from work and help me as I struggled with a raging child while trying to care for everyone else.

How our other children coped is a topic for my next book, but suffice it to say, they were devastated by what was happening to our family.

When I took our daughter to an international adoption medical clinic, I finally felt understood. There I met a doctor who was no stranger to the depth of our struggle. She knew the tests and medications our daughter needed as well as the best therapist in the region.

A Glimmer of Hope

One fall day, in total desperation, I stumbled across online videos of Dr. Karyn Purvis teaching at a small adoptive/foster parent gathering. I was glued to my computer screen as she spoke seemingly straight to me. For the first time in three years, I felt a glimmer of hope.

From the depths of my broken and fearful heart, she called forth courage.

Amid all this, Russ and I celebrated our twenty-fifth anniversary, and through a series of small miracles, we managed to get away for a few days. This was a rare, romantic time to celebrate our marriage and devote ourselves to one another, but I told Russ there was just one little thing I needed him to do—watch three lectures about children from "hard places."

This was not how he imagined spending our romantic getaway, but we watched them, held hands, and cried our way through. Dr. Purvis exuded hope—she believed children like ours could heal, so we grabbed hold of her hope and held on for dear life.

I wrote about much of this journey on my blog, *One Thankful Mom*. In the early years of writing, I believed I needed to be a voice of encouragement and hesitated to reveal the depth of our challenges. As time passed, I realized being vulnerable and transparent about our struggle and our pursuit of healing for our children would help other families. When I began writing with honesty and passion, my audience grew. We weren't alone. Other families were as desperate for help as we were.

When I discovered Dr. Purvis, I began sharing everything I was learning from her videos and her book *The Connected Child*. I was taking in so much so quickly, and I wanted everyone to know there was a way to understand and parent children who come from hard places. We could help their brains heal.

Through those posts, I developed a relationship with the folks at Empowered to Connect, a program that supports, resources, and educates caregivers, relying heavily on the Trust-Based Relational

Intervention (TBRI) model created by Dr. Purvis and Dr. David Cross. I eventually connected with Dr. Purvis herself, and later Russ and I were privileged to attend a TBRI practitioner training at Texas Christian University, where we learned even more about trust-based parenting.

Children of Trauma

As Dr. Purvis will explain, many children come from hard places, and there are many causes of trauma in children's early lives. A mother's difficult pregnancy and delivery, orphanage life, loss of parents, abuse, neglect, and other circumstances factored into my children's experiences. Your family may have experienced something entirely different, yet the impact means you, too, are parenting a child from a hard place.

As we began using our new knowledge, I yearned to know how it worked in other homes and for other families. I wanted practical, real-life examples that reflected my family. I was stumbling along, practicing the techniques Dr. Purvis taught, and I knew there must be other parents feeling just as clumsy and uncertain who might benefit from this unique blend of mommy wisdom and good science. By combining my stories of everyday life with children from hard places with Dr. Purvis's exceptional knowledge of these children, we could fill a gaping need.

This book is the meeting of scientific research with my labor of love—my family.

Dr. Purvis will explain parenting techniques, brain chemistry, and science, while I walk you through how I apply the knowledge she shares so generously.

The greatest desire of my heart is that you will be equipped and empowered to parent your children in ways that build trust, promote healing, and bring your family joy.

Many years have passed since our Ethiopian children joined our family. We've also become foster parents and have grown familiar with the hard places that children in the United States experience.

Through it all, we've learned an important truth: There are no perfect parents. You will fail many times as you parent your children, and that's okay. Give yourself grace. Reject the shaming whispers that you'll never be the parent your child needs and that you're just not good enough.

> You will fail many times as you parent your children, and that's okay. Give yourself grace.

Similarly, your children are unique individuals with their own stories. The information in this book presents many tools for your parenting tool box. Some will work well for your child, while others won't quite fit. Our children heal in their own ways and in their own time.

Keep loving, keep trying, and persevere through the hard times. You are good parents doing good work, and my heart is with you.

The Format

This book is divided into three parts. Part 1 lays a foundation for understanding attachment, which we believe is the heart of relationships. In chapter 1, Dr. Purvis explains what it means to be a child from a hard place, followed by a chapter on understanding ourselves so we can parent with healing and attachment as our goal.

Each of the seven chapters in part 2 focuses on real-life strategies that incorporate different aspects of trust-based parenting: using scripts, combatting fear, nurturing to heal, teaching respect, recognizing sensory needs, adapting strategies for teens, and building your toolbox as a parent. Part 3 is a benediction of sorts. It includes reminders of the importance of caring for yourself so you can care for your child and so you can have hope and strength for the journey ahead.

I know how tempting it is to jump ahead to part 2, but it's

important to understand the "why" so the "how" will make sense. Sure, go ahead and grab a script or sensory tip—I completely understand the need to find just one thing that might work with your child *today*—but be sure to come right back to part 1. It's worth every minute to truly understand your child.

Dr. Purvis

Throughout my life, there has always been a thread of seeking out the vulnerable. When I was a young child, it was the stray animal. I was drawn to horses that couldn't be broken and was constantly rescuing wounded birds that had fallen from their nests. As a young teen, I volunteered at a hospital as a candy striper and mentored children with learning problems. And then in college and young adulthood, I mentored and later fostered runaway teens from hard places. When I started my own family, we continued to foster children.

I married at twenty and left college, but in my forties, I decided to return to earn my degree. While at Texas Christian University, I met my mentor and colleague, Dr. David Cross. In his developmental psychology classes, I learned the science behind what I'd always done when caring for a vulnerable person or creature. Needless to say, I was smitten with the science of development, and Dr. Cross encouraged me to get my master's and doctoral degrees when I finished my undergraduate studies.

"A Nice Little Summer Camp"

During the first year of my PhD program, local adoptive parents came to us asking for help with their children who were struggling tremendously with behavioral problems. So we decided to have a summer camp both to give the parents respite and to conduct research on this small group of adoptive children. Our expectations were that we'd have a nice little summer camp, the kids would have a good time, and we would learn something about kids who had been adopted. But what actually happened started a compelling scientific and personal journey for all of us.

In that first summer camp, we just did what we knew all children need for optimal development. We saw breathtaking changes in the children in three main areas: attachment, social alertness, and language. Parents came to us after the first week in tears, saying, "My child looks into my eyes now," or "I rocked my son to sleep last night—he's never trusted me to rock him in all the years he's been home." I was stunned to see aloof children being affectionate, wary children becoming trusting, and nonverbal children exploding with language. I couldn't sleep for the rest of camp until I found the source of these profound changes.

When I was a little girl and found broken or bruised creatures, I could go ask a vet what to do and give each animal what it needed. Applying the same principle to the children who had come through our camp, I started calling my colleagues at institutions around the country to ask them why we saw such wonderful changes. What could I "feed" these precious ones to sustain such dramatic changes? Dr. T. Berry Brazelton from Harvard University returned my call and explained that by placing the children in a stabilizing environment, we had taken away violence and other maladaptive coping strategies and had given them an opportunity for optimal development.

Today we know more about why meeting needs, giving a voice, and helping regulate emotions can help a child from a hard place make up for deficits resulting from harm they experienced early in life. We have a name for what we've learned—Trust-Based Relational Intervention (TBRI)—and a method of teaching it to professionals and parents around the world.

Children Who Come from Hard Places

What do we mean when we say that a child has come from a hard place? A child from a hard place has a history of abuse, neglect, or other trauma. The trauma might have occurred before or during birth, during an early hospitalization or medical experience, in a natural disaster such as a hurricane or earthquake, or in an unhealthy relationship with a caregiver. Sadly, many children from hard places come with a unique set of challenges due to their early experiences.

If we think about the brain and body in terms of a complex computer system, we would say this is not a software issue but rather a hardware issue. When children experience trauma, their brain chemistry changes. These physical changes have a tremendous impact on their behavior. Trauma also changes children's ability to process their senses. Children may push away our hug because they have sensory processing issues. In other cases, they may be overly sensitive to noises, smells, or sounds.

Tragically, because of such trauma, these children may lose the ability to trust even the most well-intentioned, loving adults who care for them. They may be easily agitated or unable to handle stress. An individual's capacity for stress can be determined even in utero, and a mother's difficult pregnancy may cause the child to be anxious and fearful. They may also be more reactive, aggressive, and vulnerable to behavioral episodes because of the chemistry that developed in utero.

> By understanding brain development, what should have happened, and where it went wrong, parents can help their children counteract the chemistry of harm and experience a chemistry of healing.

Parents often come to us because they're perplexed and confused by their children's behaviors. The first thing I ask parents to do is to develop an awareness of the emotional, physical, and physiological changes—core development processes—that have been dramatically affected by the histories of their children. I emphasize that research shows there is great hope for every child. By understanding brain development, what *should* have happened, and where it went wrong, parents can help their children counteract the chemistry of harm and experience a chemistry of healing.

Developmental psychologists and other social researchers commonly believe that a "good enough" parent is usually more than adequate in most situations. For a child who has not experienced much harm, this is often true. But for a child who has a history of harm, the window for parenting successfully is narrower. Many common parenting techniques are actually counterproductive for the child from a hard place, and I urge parents to be selective when choosing proactive strategies that build trust with their children. When children come from hard places, their parents must be detectives, explorers, and chemists to understand the changes in each child's brain, body, biology, and belief system.

Trust-Based Relational Intervention

TBRI has as its core the goal of building an attuned, trusting relationship with a child. TBRI has three sets of principles, each considering the whole child. Many philosophies look at individual parts of the child, but we think you're most successful when you see the child holistically.

Empowering

The TBRI Empowering Principles are for the body. Children who haven't had many sensory experiences early on in their lives often need a sensory activity about every two hours. Also, children who have experienced adversity often have experienced changes in brain chemistry due to prenatal and postnatal stressors. This affects thinking, neurochemistry, and regulation of blood sugar. To meet their needs, we aim to give children a healthy, nutritious snack every two hours to support blood sugar and regulate neurochemistry.

Hydration is another important aspect of the TBRI Empowering

Principles. Children raised in an orphanage or a neglectful home probably didn't have parents following them around with a sippy cup saying, "Sweetie, do you want a sip of water?" Many children who have experienced adversity struggle with chronic dehydration, which can drive behavioral episodes and cognitive difficulties.

With respect to a child's brain chemistry, we also ask parents to empower their children by being mindful of transitions. Giving warnings between daily transitions, such as moving from one activity to another, and proactively preparing them for life transitions, such as moving to a new home or getting a new teacher, help our children feel safe and empowered.

The TBRI Empowering Principles are designed to answer the question, What are my child's physical needs, and what do they need from their environment? We want to meet physical needs so children can learn, think, and operate at their highest potentials. We want the environment to support children's learning, behavioral, and sensory needs.

Connecting

The TBRI Connecting Principles are the heart and soul of all that we are and all that we do. These principles are designed to engage with our children and to promote mindful awareness. We aim to connect to the heart of the child, to give them a voice, and to show the child that they matter. The Connecting Principles start with the caregiver. Ask yourself, "Do I look into my child's eyes? Do I touch their cheek or their arm when I talk to them? When they talk to me, do I stop what I'm doing and turn to them? Am I rushing from one thing to the next, or am I emotionally present?" We must ask ourselves these questions to be present and connect with our children.

If you think about optimal early development (something I will ask you to do many times in this book), attaching and connecting are the parent's main focus during the child's first year of life. Parents spend countless hours holding, touching, gazing at, and talking to their precious children. However, many children did not have this experience, so the TBRI Connecting Principles empower parents to build bridges to their children. Regardless of whether the children are newborns or two or twelve, they all need the same thing when they come to us: connection. The goal of the TBRI Connecting Principles is to build trust so we can connect to children's hearts and build trusting relationships.

Correcting

Lastly, the TBRI Correcting Principles are designed to shape the beliefs and behaviors of our children. Because of their histories, many children from hard places act out of fear because they believe they must be in control of their environments if they are to survive. By empowering and connecting with our children, we can disarm fear and guide them toward more desirable behaviors. With these principles, we help parents learn how to redirect their child's behavior while still being deeply empowering and deeply connected caregivers. We ask parents to be both proactive and responsive as they address their child's behavior. They can be proactive by teaching skills when the child is calm and alert and his physical needs are met. When parents respond to problematic behaviors, we ask them to see the need behind those behaviors and respond to them at an appropriate level. We provide many examples throughout this book of how to do just that.

In summary, these are the three things we aim to do with every child we serve:

- We meet physical needs with food, water, and sensory input.
- We meet connection needs by putting the relationship at the focus of every interaction.

- We correct behavior and thinking by disarming fear, allowing the authentic child beneath to emerge.

Because the harm our children have experienced is often holistic, we must address challenges with holistic interventions. By employing strategies to empower their bodies, connect to their spirits, and correct their beliefs and behaviors, we can effectively help our children come to deep healing.

Parenting your child this way may sound daunting. We often call it "investment parenting" because we must devote so much time, energy, and personal connection to build trust. This type of parenting will likely cost you most in the beginning because both you and your child are still learning. Just like plowing an untouched field, the first time you introduce trust-based parenting will always be the toughest. But every time you plow the field after that, it gets easier. We've found that even in short periods of time, holistic, trust-based parenting can yield great gains, starting the path to intense, joyful healing. This healing is not only for the child but for parents as well. In my many years spent caring for the vulnerable, I've found the rewards that come from this type of parenting far outweigh the costs.

It's easy to feel alone on this journey and misunderstood as a parent. I urge you to find people who understand your family who can support you, encourage you, and hold you accountable. Find safe people you can lean on as you walk the path to healing.

My greatest hope for you is that beneath your child's behaviors you'll find the real child, the child who is precious, who wants to connect, who wants desperately to be loved—but who has had to protect their heart from their history.

Lisa

This book was written over the course of many years. Many of the stories I share were written when my children were young. Today, as the mother of middle-schoolers, teens, and young adults, I continue to apply the knowledge behind these stories each day. With some adaptation, the techniques work for kids of all ages.

When my teens share stories about particular classmates after a day at school, I often point them toward an understanding of the student's history. Perhaps the boy has challenges with impulsivity because of the way his brain functions. Maybe the girl behaves the way she does because her early childhood experiences led to a deep need to control her environment.

Understanding the impact of a person's early life and traumas, whether small or large, changes the way we see people. We have greater compassion for one another in our marriages and friendships.

If I could go back to the beginning of my mothering journey and parent all my children focusing on trust and connection, I would. Thankfully, my children extend a lot of grace to me, and I love them more than I can express in these pages.

Key Takeaways

- Children from hard places suffer a variety of adverse experiences, including abuse, neglect, and trauma. Because this population is so diverse, we may also use the terms "children who have experienced adversity," "children with a history of harm," "children who have experienced trauma," or "vulnerable children."

- There is hope for healing with intentional, holistic intervention.

- Many traditional parenting methods are not effective with children who have experienced trauma.

- Trust-Based Relational Intervention (TBRI) aims to meet the needs of children in three ways:

  1. *Empowering*: We meet physical needs with food, water, and sensory input.

  2. *Connecting*: We meet connection needs by focusing on the relationship in every interaction.

  3. *Correcting*: We correct behavior and thinking by disarming fear, allowing the authentic child beneath to emerge.

- Children from hard places often have holistic needs because many developmental processes have been interrupted by adversity in childhood. Therefore, they require holistic intervention.

Part 1

The
Heart of
Relationships

1

Understand the Foundation
of Attachment

Lisa

After thirty hours of travel, we arrived home from Ethiopia with a five-month-old infant and a nearly two-year-old child. By 2007, we'd had seven children by birth, and now we were ready to parent these new little ones. We knew they had experienced loss. They had been separated from their first parents, and more relationships had been broken when we took them from their orphanage. Our goals were to meet their needs, keep them close, and show them again and again that they could trust us.

This process is the foundation of attachment. A baby cries to express a need, a parent meets the need, and the baby is calmed. We had done this for many years with our biological children, and they never doubted our presence and comfort.

Our new little ones had already lost the dearest figures in their lives: their mothers. I can only imagine the confusion and deep sadness this must have caused in their minds and hearts.

Then they went to an orphanage where the nannies genuinely cared for the children but where there were many children with many needs and only a small number of caregivers. These caregivers also changed throughout the day and night. I imagine some were gentle, providing comfort, while others were more businesslike. These children were not theirs, but the job provided food for their own children at home.

Once we arrived back home in Idaho, we slept with the boys either next to our bed or cuddled up next to us. I fed our youngest nearly exclusively, holding him against my skin as I gave him a bottle. Most of the time, I was able to do the same with our toddler.

We kept them close, wearing them in baby carriers as much as possible. We wanted them to feel our presence, hear our heartbeats, and know our voices.

The older kids were excited and wanted to help. Exhausted from lack of sleep, one night I woke to find the baby was not in his crib next to me. I was terrified for a moment, but then I looked into the room shared by my teen daughters and found him in the arms of my eighteen-year-old, both asleep.

Building Attachment

We made eye contact with the boys, talked to them, sang songs, and provided comfort. One of our boys looked right back into our eyes, smiling and engaging. The other was more hesitant. He didn't like eye contact, but he would let me hold him close as I read books or gave him a bottle. With so many losses in his life, he wasn't eager to trust me.

When he was two and a half, he followed his teen brother into our pasture, where he stepped on a yellow jacket nest and was swarmed. We were all terrified as we tried to rescue him while also surrounded by stinging insects ourselves. We were stung many times, but our little guy suffered the most, with thirty-five stings.

Saddest to me was that he did not want my comfort. The pain was great, but our attachment wasn't yet strong enough for him to turn to me in that

> Our job is to prove ourselves trustworthy again and again... and again.

moment. We bathed him and gave him medicine. We tried to comfort him, but he pushed us away and wanted to be put in his crib. Now, years later, tears fill my eyes as I share this with you.

Building attachment with a child who has lost his or her primary caregiver takes time. Our job is to prove ourselves trustworthy again and again...and again. This repetition is exhausting, and sometimes we fail. But we keep building on the foundation we're establishing, one positive interaction at a time, until we've created an attachment relationship for our children to build on for the rest of their lives.

Dr. Purvis

The Attachment Cycle

Attachment is an affectionate bond between a caregiver and a youngster—an infant, child, or adolescent. It's the bond that tells that child they're safe, their needs matter, and they are precious. Within the attachment bond, the caregiver acts as the external regulator for all the child's needs.

For several decades, we have understood what is called the "attachment cycle," which essentially says that a baby cries and a caregiver comes, and a baby cries again and a caregiver comes again. This cycle happens over and over...and over and over. And a child learns, "If I have a need and I cry, someone comes and tenderly meets that need."

So if the child is hungry, the caregiver brings food. If the child is cold, the caregiver brings warmth. If a child is lonely, the caregiver brings a soft shoulder and a lullaby to rock them to sleep. This external regulation and the giving of nurture make us human. All that is beautiful and glorious about us as human beings develops in the arms of attachment. The child learns not only that they're precious but also that they have a voice—when they cry, somebody shows up. The child learns that their needs *matter*.

We often call this pattern "the giving of yeses" because when you think about development, the parents essentially say yes for the child's first two years of life. A baby cries because she's hungry, and her parent says, "Yes, I will feed you" and meets that need. A baby cries because she's cold, and her parent says, "Yes, I will warm you" as they hold their little one.

"Yes, I will comfort you."

"Yes, I will cradle you."

"Yes, I will sing to you."

In fact, it isn't until the child is about two years of age that they might take a dangerous object toward the electric socket and we have to say our first no.

This giving of yeses happens hundreds of thousands of times in the earliest years of life. The baby cries, and the caregiver comes. The child learns that their needs are going to be met, so they learn trust. This is the lesson of the first year of life—"I can trust." A child learns to connect to their caregivers because they know Mommy or Daddy will come, bringing food, warmth, love, snuggles, or dry diapers. In addition to establishing trust, the repeated completions of this cycle lay a strong foundation for self-worth, self-efficacy (the child knows he has a voice), self-regulation, and mental health.

Attachment and Brain Chemistry

Research from the past twenty years about the attachment cycle is sobering. When a child cries and no one comes, the child's brain chemistry is dramatically altered. There are so many children in our society and globally who have come from hard places of neglect, abuse, or trauma. They've suffered so many hardships, and their capacities to trust have been fiercely damaged. It's critical to remember a child who has come from a hard place didn't get a lot of yeses. Their needs were not met in their earliest days, so they lack the experiences that build the foundation for trust. As a result, there are dramatic altera-tions in their belief system about the world.

In optimal development, most children will grow up believing, "The world is a safe place. I'm going to be loved and cared for." But sadly, that is not the case with the child who has experienced relational trauma. Research tells us a child's ability to handle stress and to self-regulate as well as their later mental health can all be predicted by their early attachment relationships.[1] When the child's needs are not met, the result is chronic, toxic stress that can start a trajectory for mental health challenges. In early childhood, this may look like behavior dysregulation. As the child starts school, it may present as ADD/ADHD diagnoses or symptoms. And into adolescence, if these children aren't given holistic intervention, they may experience depression, anxiety, or other psychiatric problems.

A man once approached me after I'd finished a speaking engagement and said, "You know, you're not telling me anything my grandmother didn't know. This attachment stuff isn't rocket science!" And he was right! I believe parents, grandparents, and great-grandparents have understood for generations that it's important for children to have parents who adore, love, and care for them. But recent developments in science have given us a more sophisticated ability to measure brain development in children. We now have the "rocket science" to support what generations before us have always known.

Dependence and Autonomy

Research clearly shows that children must be very, very dependent when they're young in order to be truly independent, or "autonomous," when they're older.[2] Little children from hard places who haven't learned to trust may look independent, but they are actually pseudo-independent. Someone without knowledge of attachment may even praise this trait, thinking these children are developmentally advanced, but sadly, this pseudoindependence is a marker that these children don't have the internal capacities to form relationships or deep trust. Whatever age a child comes to us, they need to be fully dependent on us in the beginning. For how long? you may ask. That depends on many factors, and it's not predicted by their chronological age.

One of the most scientifically weighty documents to be published in recent years on the subject of attachment is *Hardwired to Connect*, by the Commission on Children at Risk. In it, dozens of the most notable scientists of our age looked at early childhood development. They discovered that recent research confirms what we've known for years: Little ones are hardwired to connect from birth. They are intuitively, instinctively desperate to look into the eyes of their caregivers. If you put a newborn on their mommy's tummy, they will intuitively, instinctively crawl up to the breast and attach. And they will look through their bleary newborn vision for the face of their caregiver. We are made for connection. We are hardwired for connection. And if a loving connection fails, all development fails with it.

> We are made for connection. We are hardwired for connection. And if a loving connection fails, all development fails with it.

We know that the brain of a child who has a secure attachment relationship to a safe, loving adult is dramatically different from the brain of a child who does not. All capacities in the brain are dramatically altered when there is no safe adult on duty. Fight, flight, or freeze systems are provoked much more easily if no caregiver is on duty.

Complex Developmental Trauma

For many years, a diagnosis of reactive attachment disorder (RAD) meant, "These traits tell us this child didn't have an attachment figure, and these are now simply behavioral attachment strategy traits." But recent neuroscience has proven that the child's brain was instead dramatically altered. Every trait we had previously called a behavioral reactive attachment strategy has now been proven to be tied to brain development and the behavioral systems that failed.

A new diagnosis has been proposed and is being embraced by researchers, scientists, and psychologists all over the world: complex developmental trauma. This diagnosis takes neuroscience into account as it relates to attachment. In complex developmental trauma, brain development is deeply impacted by repeated relational trauma sustained as a child. Because of ruptured early relationships, all a child's systems are different, including how this child feels, how they think, how they learn, how they process the senses, and how they interact with peers. Every region of the child's brain that deals with the substance of life has been altered. It is a harm with global implications for the child's development. Children who have been harmed in this way need a holistic environment that is mindful of this global impact.

Attachment and Behavior

So you might be asking, What does this look like behaviorally? There are some common symptoms of attachment problems, and very often they have to do with a child pushing away from a caregiver's touch or hug. This looks like rejecting care or nurture, just as the response of Lisa's son did when he was stung by yellow jackets. A child may not look into others' eyes unless they want something. There are many reasons these things happen, and one of them is that the child's brain development was altered.

Trust and Control

The behavioral strategies children use give us clues to help us identify issues with trust. Perhaps a child uses a great deal of manipulation or control, aggression, or violence to get their needs met. This child may steal food from the kitchen rather than asking for food because they were hungry before they came to your family. A child who struggles with attachment does not yet know they can ask for their needs to be met. This child may triangulate and try to work the caregivers against one another. Quite simply, the child has not learned to trust, which is the essence of attachment.

Again, remember that the brain of a human infant is designed for three years of mentoring by the brain of a loving adult. The only way a child learns empathy, compassion, and self-regulation is by external regulation and then co-regulation. The behavioral symptoms we see stemming from attachment needs are simply strategies for the child to meet their own needs. Their behavior depends greatly on whether the child feels safe enough and empowered to use words.

Many of the parents we work with describe their child as controlling. These children are afraid to let anyone else control their worlds. They believe they would have died if they had not tried to stay in control, and sadly, for many of these children, it is true. Because of early harm, abuse, or neglect, they learned survival strategies to feel safe and in control and, in some cases, to stay alive. To expect these same children to trust us and give up those strategies is a huge request.

"How Can I Say Yes?"

Naturally, these behaviors can be extremely distressing to parents who long to connect to the heart of the child they've brought home. Parents can easily take this behavior personally, but I always urge them to understand complex developmental trauma so they can understand and respect the reasons their child's homecoming may not be as magical as they'd hoped. Remember that in an optimal environment, as an infant, this child would have asked for a need by crying. And you would have said yes hundreds of thousands of times before he or she was two years old.

For example, let's say you have a child who comes to your home from foster care at the age of eight. Because of this child's background, he didn't get two years of yeses. To help make up for this deficit and build trust, you must find creative ways to say yes. So we explore the possibilities with parents and encourage them to ask themselves, "What are a dozen ways I can say yes?" In later chapters of this book, we'll discuss topics such as giving voice, choices, and compromises—all powerful ways to build trust and a relationship with your child. The giving of yeses and the meeting of physical needs were how trust was originally earned. Regardless of the age of the child in your home, these are still the pathways to trust, brain development, and a healthy relationship with your child. A yes for a two-year-old will look different for a twelve-year-old, but the principle is the same.

Beyond Addressing Behavior

Parents often become frustrated because their children act so much younger than their chronological ages. However, we know from a research study by Becker-Weidman that if a child's brain didn't develop in a typical way, they have the brain of a child that is half their age or even younger.[3] So an eight-year-old child may act like they are four or even three years old. Please don't be annoyed with your child's seemingly babyish behaviors. Instead, take them back to the place of early development and meet those earliest, most primitive and important needs for attachment, safety, and trust.

Of course, it is completely understandable for a parent to be concerned about their child's behavioral challenges. Obviously we must address behaviors, but making behavior the only mark of a child's success can cause even more problems. The most important goal is connection. If we gain connection and a trusting relationship, the behaviors we desire will follow. If we address a behavior with the goal of earning trust, not of correcting the behavior to look good, the relationship flourishes, and good behavior will grow from that.

Simply put, relationship-based traumas require relationship-based healings. This means we must be intentional about making up for what our child lost in their early days and re-creating what they should have experienced in optimal development. As you explore what your child missed in their history, it's equally important for you to dig into your own history, as this is the greatest predictor of your child's ability to attach. We'll discuss adult attachment in the next chapter.

Lisa

As I mentioned in the introduction, in addition to our little boys, we adopted two girls from Ethiopia, one in 2007 and another in 2008.

Our younger daughter spent her days on the streets of the poorest slum in Ethiopia and experienced severe neglect. She cried, but nobody came. She was terribly hungry but not fed. When there was food, it was given to more favored children. She was cold, but there were no blankets.

Numerous implicit memories were formed:

- I cry and nobody comes—I'm alone.

- I'm hungry—I will probably die.

- People are dangerous—I must not trust them. I'll take care of myself.

- There isn't enough—I must get as much food, attention, and affection as I can.

How could we help her make sense of her overwhelming reactions to hunger, fear of trusting and attaching to parents, and a deep sense of competition with siblings?

When a child cries and nobody comes, or is hungry and not fed, the child begins to see the world (including adults) as untrustworthy and unpredictable. When my daughter needed comfort but was left to herself, her fear increased, and her brain was rewired to view the world as erratic and unsafe.

This chronic fear coursed through my daughter's veins, coloring her world. Her responses to seemingly small problems were huge and often out of control. She was unable to calm herself and refused to let us comfort her. She was hypervigilant, constantly watching for danger lurking around every corner. Likewise, she saw the world as unfair and constantly sought to meet her own needs by asserting herself against her siblings.

I learned she was desperate for my attention and would do whatever was necessary to get it. If good behavior didn't work, she would do her best to disrupt the day. Any attention is better than no attention for a child who has suffered from such profound neglect.

It took years of repetition and professional intervention to help our child's brain heal. The work was harder than we could ever have imagined, but we gave it all we had.

Learning to Care

Some of our children came to us certain that they didn't need parents at all. They had learned to take care of themselves and meet their own needs. In time, they grew to care about us. I recall a day when my daughter was sitting across the counter from me, doing homework as I cooked.

"Mom, you're so pretty," she said.

"Why, thank you," I replied. "That's very sweet of you."

"I love you, Mom."

"I love you too."

"When I first met you, I didn't care about you yet, and I didn't really like you, but now I love you and think you're pretty. Do you think if another mom had come for me, I would have loved her too and thought she was pretty?"

I thought for a moment. "I think I'm exactly the right mom who was supposed to come for you. I was meant to be your mom. It took time, but we were meant to love each other."

Does it look like the attachment relationship I have with some of my other children? No it doesn't, but it's still good.

I'll close with this story about one of my young daughters.

One summer night after a long day filled with activity, we arrived home, and the kids were extremely tired. They had played hard all day, returned home to have a snack and do chores, and then gone back out for a fun evening.

My daughter plopped down in a big chair with a sad look on her face. I asked, "Do you want me to hold you?"

"No." She looked away. "I want to go home."

"Home? We *are* home. Let's get you ready for bed."

"I want to go home to Ethiopia."

I paused to wrap my mind around this. "Well, it would be wonderful to go to Ethiopia, but not all of your family is there anymore."

"My Ethiopia mommy died."

"Yes, honey, she died."

"Why didn't my mommy give me a family in Ethiopia?" She paused again. "Do other kids get new families when their mommies die?"

She crawled into my lap, and I rocked her while she sat stiffly with her back to my chest.

"Yes, you have lots of friends who got new families after their mommies died. Lots of kids you know have new families who adopted them after their parents died." I hugged her. "Your Ethiopia mommy loved you so much—you were precious to her. We love you too, and I'm so glad to be your mommy."

She snuggled in closer and rested her head on my shoulder.

Sometimes attachment builds slowly over months and years. Other times it seems to come more quickly and naturally. As parents, our job is to love faithfully and seek ways to build this bond with our children. It's been my experience that if you adopt multiple children, it will look and feel different with each one.

And that's okay.

Key Takeaways

- Attachment is an affectionate bond between a caregiver and child.

- As caregivers meet young babies' needs, they establish a foundation of trust that has positive effects throughout the life span.

- Conversely, when a child's needs are not met early in life, they experience toxic stress, which can set them on a trajectory of mental illness.

- A child must be dependent early in life in order to become independent later in life.

- Complex developmental trauma accounts for the impact of attachment deficits on brain development.

- Children from hard places often have a developmental age that is half or less of their biological age. For example, a nine-year-old may act like a four-year-old.

Try It Today

Write down three to five ways you can practice giving your child a yes, and try them out throughout the week.

2

Know Yourself

Lisa

Just as our children don't arrive as blank slates, we come to parenting with our own unique histories. Let's be honest—even the best childhood is not completely free of hardship.

When I think back to my childhood, I'm a bit stunned to realize that even those in my small crowd of friends had their share of traumas with a capital "T": the death of a parent, a mother with cancer, parental divorce, teen pregnancy, substance abuse, depression, suicidal thoughts, eating disorders, bullying, and chronic anxiety are just some of the challenges that come to mind.

More common challenges (traumas with a little "t") impact children as well. These include things such as children moving houses, dating and breaking up, and simply not feeling like they belong. A therapist friend shared that she sees many children for whom moving is a significant trauma. I find this comforting because moving from the city to a small town in late elementary school was very difficult for me. I lost my bearings for a long time.

Attachment and Your Family History

How my friends and I coped with our "big T" and "little t" traumas had a lot to do with our attachment to our parents. Those of us who had a secure attachment and whose parents provided a secure base probably weathered the hardest parts of childhood far better than our friends who didn't have reliable support.

Some parents who decide to adopt or care for foster children have experienced severe challenges in their childhoods. Abuse, neglect, and adoption losses may be part of your own childhood story.

Think back to your childhood. How were you parented? Did you experience safety and consistency from caring, healthy parents? Did you know you were precious and loved?

Or were your parents distant, showing little emotion and affection? Did you seek assurance from other adults, like teachers? Were your friends your primary support and safe base?

Did you have parents who were inconsistent—sometimes affectionate and meeting your needs, while the next day ignoring you and leaving you to figure things out on your own? When you cried or were having a hard time, were you unsure which version of your parent would show up to help, if they did at all?

Did you have parents with addictions or mental health challenges?

The parenting we experienced continues to influence us into adulthood and in our own parenting. It gets even more interesting when we blend our attachment history with our partner's. This may sound discouraging, but I have good news: We aren't trapped in our childhood attachment patterns and styles.

Your Life Narrative

What happened to us as children is not as important as *how we've made sense of it* as adults. We can't change our experiences, but when we're able to step back and view ourselves and our parents with compassion and insight, we form our "life narrative."

You can form secure attachments with your spouse and children even if you didn't have secure attachments with your parents.

Even more hopeful, this attachment healing doesn't need to come from your relationship with a parent. A safe connection with another trustworthy, attuned adult can change your own attachment trajectory. A teacher, extended family member, pastor, or other person who becomes a safe base can make all the difference.

I know a young man who grew up in a profoundly neglectful home. His family history included generations of addiction and abuse. He followed his parents' footsteps into the world of drug addiction, and like the generations before him, he landed in jail. This was not uncommon for people in his family and came as no big surprise.

> What happened to us as children is not as important as how we've made sense of it as adults.

While in jail, he reflected on the one stable relationship in his life: the one he shared with his grandparents on his father's side. They were a consistent, safe presence and his secure base in a tumultuous world. When life at home became unbearable, he moved in with them. When home got better, he moved back in with his parents. This cycle repeated itself many times.

Now, as an older teen, he knew he didn't want to follow the path of his parents. He wanted a life like his grandparents'. Although they didn't have a lot of money, there was plenty of food, the utilities weren't turned off due to lack of payment, and drugs and alcohol were not part of the daily diet.

This young man is an overcomer.

His attachment to his parents was far from secure, but he formed a secure attachment with his grandparents. Over and over they met his needs. They became his secure base.

He is also intentionally creating a different childhood for his younger siblings and, someday, his own children. He desires to meet their needs time and time again, just as his grandparents met his. He plans to be their secure base and is already demonstrating it with his younger brothers.

Just as he is changing the course of his family's history, we can change the course of ours.

Triggers

In addition to understanding attachment, we need to be aware of our triggers. Parents often identify their children's triggers—the things that start a downward behavior spiral. We have triggers too, and sometimes they really get in the way of being the parents we want to be.

If disrespect makes your head feel like it might explode, explore it and be curious about your feelings. What about your child being disrespectful really bothers you? When you reflect on your childhood, do these feelings seem to make sense? Then learn to manage it with healthy coping skills. If you're adopting or fostering older kids, you can nearly count on a lack of respect.

How about rejection by your child? Are you overly sensitive due to rejection in your own life? Do you find yourself desperate for your child's acceptance? Or do you turn away because they don't seem to want your love anyhow?

My child once told me I would never be able to help anyone because I wasn't a good mom and I couldn't help her. Her words went straight to my heart, pulling up feelings of failure and inadequacy.

My mind told me it was her pain talking, but my heart felt it deeply. This was a trigger for me. I wanted to back away, shield my heart, and protect myself. But those coping mechanisms don't lead to connection. Knowing this was a trigger, acknowledging it, and reminding myself of the truth helped me stay present with my child.

There are so many things that can pull us back into our childhood experiences. Our traumas and attachments to our parents or other adults do not have to determine the parents we become. How we make sense of it can make all the difference.

Dr. Purvis

At our institute, parents who are struggling in their relationships with their children often lament that their child won't attach to them. These parents have a deep longing to have the kind of connection with their children that they see some of their friends and peers enjoying in their families. They are heartbroken when they experience disconnection and rejection from their children. Perhaps you've had a similar experience in your family. If so, I'd like to extend this gentle invitation: Explore where you have come from and discover the messages you are sending to your children by the way you parent.

Back to the Beginning

Throughout this book, Lisa and I will often remind you to "go back to the beginning" of your child's experience. We'll ask you to consider the deficits your child felt in their early life, and we'll provide tools that will help you make up for those losses. In this chapter, we are asking you to do the same for yourself. To bring a child to a place of healing, you must know the path yourself. Many parents have never explored their own paths to healing, and some may even be unaware they are carrying wounds from childhood.

Most parents are not aware of their own attachment styles. We seem to think that because it's in our past, it no longer affects us. But in reality, every one of us speaks some words we've heard spoken, or we do some things to our children that were done to us when we were children. Every one of us has unconscious parenting strategies that become apparent when we reflect on the parenting we received. As we become insightful about our histories, we will probably choose to let go of some parenting strategies so that we can be most effective with our own children.

> To bring a child to a place of healing, you must know the path yourself.

Unless a parent has examined their own childhood and upbringing, they're likely to carry out those same patterns with their own children and repeat the same errors their parents may have made. Our purpose in asking parents to explore their histories is to help them be mindful and emotionally present and then to bring a deep, rich healing presence to their relationships with their children.

Identifying Our Attachment Style

Research is clear that the most dynamic and powerful predictor of a child's attachment style is their caregiver's attachment style.[1] If a caregiver is warm, nurturing, and emotionally available, the child's outcome will be dramatically different from that of a child who may have received instrumental care but little nurturing.

Selma Fraiberg has performed classic research on what she calls the "ghosts in the nursery."[2] This striking metaphor reminds us that a shadow of the parenting we received as children falls over the cradles and cribs of our own young. Fraiberg frequently says that "as parents, we do unto others as we were done unto." When parents are reflective about their childhood histories, it makes a dramatic change in how they parent.

Our colleagues at Circle of Security, an attachment intervention program for parents, describe this phenomenon as "shark music." Imagine you are looking at a peaceful ocean view. Suddenly you hear those infamous two notes that immediately make you think of the movie *Jaws*. In that moment, the serene ocean scene becomes a danger zone riddled with sharks. Our shark music is made of feelings from our own childhood experiences that impact our current relationship with our children. Parents can learn to identify their shark music by exploring their childhood experiences and attachment histories.

The Adult Attachment Interview (AAI) is the gold standard of research-based adult attachment standards. If you can find a clinician who is trained in the AAI, I urge you to utilize that resource. If you're not able to access the AAI, working with a therapist well trained in attachment should lead you to the same insights.

We won't be diving into the four major attachment styles in this book, but we will focus on the general categories of secure and insecure attachment and provide insights that will help you begin to identify where you fall on the spectrum.

Four Skills for Meaningful Relationships

One way I ask parents to explore their histories is by reflecting on the skills one develops through meaningful relationships, as outlined by Jude Cassidy in her article "Truth, Lies, and Intimacy: An Attachment Perspective."[3] This article synthesizes what we know about attachment and presents four skills that are required to establish meaningful relationships and attachments into adulthood—in other words, secure attachments. They're four simple skills, but taken in sum, they're dynamic and powerful.

1. We must be able to give care. What I mean is nurturing, loving care—not just instrumental care. For example, if your child is hurt, do you simply remind him where the Band-Aids are, or do you help him take care of his wound, hold him, and look into his eyes and tell him you're so sorry he was hurt?

2. We must be able to receive care from others without pushing them away or ignoring our needs. Do you allow people to help you meet your needs? How easily do you accept acts of kindness from others?

3. We need to know the autonomous self. This means being able to find contentment in solitude or with others. It also refers to the ability to know yourself and make choices based on your needs. Do you feel anxious and

insecure even during appropriate times away from your loved ones? Are you able to identify your own needs and desires outside your relationship with another person?

4. We must be able to negotiate needs. Just as you teach your children to use their words, how easily can you voice your needs in an acceptable way?

Ability in these four skills predicts satisfying, meaningful relationships for adults in their attachment relationships. I often encourage parents to spend time honestly reflecting on their faculties in these four skills. Which of the skills come easily for *you*? Which are more difficult? Asking a counselor, spouse, family member, or trusted friend to give their insights as you reflect can also be helpful.

The Path to Healing

I want to start by saying that the parents I have worked with over the years are, by and large, wonderful and ferociously protective parents. No matter what their attachment style might be, there is no question that they love their children deeply. The truth of the matter is that we're all human. We can all learn from our own histories, and we can all parent our children more joyfully and effectively in light of this knowledge.

Looking Back to Move Forward

I often say that it is only as I heal my own history that I can know the right path to lead a child to heal their own history. So if you can't go to your own sadness, you can't lead your son to his. If you can't go to your own fear, you can't lead your daughter to hers. If you can't go to your own loss, you can't lead your teenager to theirs. If you were harmed, it's important to acknowledge and grieve that harm. If you had a parent who was an alcoholic, you must grieve trying to fix him or her and not being able to do it. If you've had losses as a young adult, you need to grieve those losses before you can help your child make sense of their own. It is only in the grieving and the owning of our history that we can move forward with a clear view of the child standing before us. As you begin this arduous, important work, I urge you to find a trusted professional, such as a licensed counselor or social worker, to help you process your history.

Once you've identified the areas of relationships that are more difficult for you, it's important to press even deeper and learn why this is the case. The reason I want to help parents go to these places is not to shame or blame them for their children's struggles but so they can guide children to that same place of healing.

Here is a simplified example that resonates with many parents with whom I've worked: After reflecting on your history, perhaps you've realized that giving nurturing care is difficult for you. As you explore your past, maybe you realize that even though your parents were wonderful people, they struggled to be nurturing when you needed it. As a result, you may find it difficult to give nurturing care beyond instrumental care when your child is hurt or upset. Big displays of emotion may feel uncomfortable for you because your needs were not met as a child. Furthermore, situations in which you feel that your emotions are dismissed are very difficult for you. Parents with this experience often find that disrespect from their children is a huge trigger because it makes them feel dismissed, just as they did when they were young children in need of nurturing care. This is just one example of how our childhood experiences impact our relationships as adults. It's important to become mindful of these experiences so we can change the same trajectory for our children.

Becoming Mindful

Learning to be mindful is a marathon, not a sprint. Please understand that building mindful awareness takes time. Please be kind to yourself, patient with yourself, and forgiving of yourself. Like all new skills, we learn by trial and error.

Start by taking a few minutes several times a day, and just focus on the last interaction you had with your child. Notice the dilation of your child's pupils, their tone of voice, and whether they turn away from you or toward you. Use these physical clues to focus on what's going on with your child.

Then focus on your reaction. Do you feel chaotic and confused by what your child said or how she reacted? Do you feel defensive? That's okay. Accept those feelings, and try to breathe through what makes you uncomfortable. Try to stay present as you feel these difficult emotions.

This practice will help you begin to identify your triggers, as Lisa mentioned. Going back to the example I gave above, if your child is disrespectful and rolls his eyes at you, you might feel defensive or angry. But if you can breathe through those feelings and remain present to your child, you can remember what he has experienced and how he learned to use disrespect to defend himself from harm. Keeping this in mind, you can say gently, firmly, and without losing control, "Son, I'm listening. Please say that again with respect."

If you begin to practice purposeful attention in short stints, gradually increasing their duration and frequency, it can become second nature. When you develop the muscle of mindfulness, you can be more present to your children. You don't have to let your history sweep you away into a battle or power struggle with your child. Mindfulness is cultivated like any new skill—gradually. Eventually, it will positively impact every relationship in our lives.

There Is Hope

Perhaps you've never explored your own attachment history. May I gently say that until you do, it will be very difficult to bring the child before you to a place of deep healing? Go ahead and take a deep breath. This is difficult work we're asking you to do, but it is critical for the well-being of your child.

The hopeful message is that everyone can change. All of us can be more available, more mindful, more emotionally present—first to ourselves as we give a voice to our own histories, and then to our children. I have worked with children with psychiatric diagnoses and attachment diagnoses all over the world, and I have never met a single child who couldn't experience dramatic levels of healing. However, these children must have a nurturing environment with an insightful caregiver who has explored their own history so they can lead their child toward a path of healing.

Lisa

My friend Jenn grew up in a family where achievement was highly valued. Any grade below an A was considered a sign of laziness. Her parents always seemed disappointed in her.

She did not maintain a 4.0, but she was a good student. She chose to move across the country for college and changed her major a few times, trying to find the right balance of ambition and happiness. Her parents were disappointed to discover she was no longer planning a prestigious career and thought she was settling for something easier.

Jenn met Mark in her sophomore American literature class. He was kind and committed. She felt safe and comfortable with him.

They married after graduation, and two years later had their first child, Henry. He was a fussy baby, and Jenn often worried she wasn't meeting his needs very well. Sometimes she couldn't figure out how to comfort him, but most of the time, she felt she did a good job.

One summer day, they took a hike with Henry in the backpack. A sunhat covered his nearly bald head and shielded his face from the sun. Henry fell asleep as they walked the trail. When they got back to the trailhead, Jenn noticed that Henry's head had tipped to the side and left his cheek uncovered and exposed to the sun. His red cheek seemed to be a sign of her failure. Surely a good mom wouldn't allow her baby to get sunburned.

Mark assured her it was simply an accident, but she was ashamed of what she perceived as her failure. A good friend saw Henry the next day and jokingly said, "Bad mama!" This struck Jenn's heart with unreasonable force. She turned away with tears in her eyes.

Two years later they had a second son, Luke. He was smiley, happy, and easy to console. He nursed well and loved being cuddled. Henry adored him most of the time, and the transition to a family of four seemed pretty easy.

Jenn and Mark enjoyed their little family and loved being parents. Several years had passed when they read an article in the local paper and became aware of the need for foster parents in their community. They attended an information meeting to learn more about foster care and decided that becoming foster parents was something they could do.

They had a sweet family. Their boys were doing well in kindergarten and second grade, and life was ticking along nicely. Mark and Jenn enjoyed children and knew this was a good fit for them. Maybe they would even adopt a child they fostered. Who knew?

The process of becoming licensed took longer than they expected. The training was good, but they were a little surprised by how detailed the home study was. Jenn was frustrated by the amount of information the caseworker wanted about her childhood. That all happened years ago; why did it matter so much? She was an adult now, and she had great relationships with her parents and siblings.

Mark and Jenn's first placement was a six-year-old girl. This little one wouldn't let Jenn touch her—only Mark could feed her or brush her hair before school. If Mark wasn't home, she tried to do everything herself and would scream at Jenn, "Go away! I hate you!"

Jenn had learned enough to know this was not uncommon, but she was surprised by how much it hurt her. After weeks of this, she felt completely rejected. When the screaming started, she began to think to herself, "That's okay, I think I might hate you too." She was ashamed of her thoughts and couldn't confess this to anyone. This little girl had been hurt by the parents who were supposed to protect her. Her behavior was not surprising. Still, Jenn felt daggers in her heart as the child continued to reject her, wanting only Mark.

It took Mark's help for Jenn to begin untangling her feelings. He knew her, loved her, and understood her heart. This experience led Jenn to begin learning more about herself and exploring her reactions. She decided she wanted the help of a counselor.

After four months (although it felt much longer), Jenn's foster daughter began to trust her a little. She let Jenn brush her hair without screaming and hiding. She sat closer when Jenn read books aloud. One day she asked Jenn to show her how to make a peanut butter and jelly sandwich. Jenn pulled a chair up to the counter for her foster daughter, and with laughter and a little mess, they made a sandwich together. Jenn found herself feeling a connection with her foster daughter that she hadn't felt before. She relaxed into the warmth of it.

Though Jenn's daughter sometimes continued to reject her and yell "I hate you," Jenn was able to keep her emotions in check, knowing this was about the child's big feelings and fears, not her own. She grew to love this little girl and was sad to say goodbye when the little girl was reunified with her biological family.

Exploring her childhood and relationship with her parents gave Jenn insight into her struggles with her foster daughter. As Dr. Purvis says, she had to "look back in order to move forward." This was not a quick fix or easy process but was worth every counseling session, every tearful conversation with Mark, and even the discomfort of realizing her parents were only human too. They did the best they could do with what they knew, and now Jenn could build on their efforts. She knew she could be a better mom to all her kids with this new knowledge.

Key Takeaways

- To bring your child to a place of healing, you must know the path yourself.

- Four skills for meaningful relationships:

    1. *Give care.* How easily are you able to give care without resentment or discomfort?

    2. *Receive care.* How easily are you able to receive care from others?

    3. *Negotiate needs.* How easily are you able to identify and negotiate your needs in a relationship?

    4. *Be autonomous.* How comfortable are you being independent?

Try It Today

- Begin a journaling practice to explore your history. Reflect on your own relationship with your parents or caregivers. How might these relationships be impacting your relationship with your child?

- Set aside five minutes each day of a week to practice mindfulness. Reflect on the last interaction you had with your child, and journal your experience, using the prompts on page 55-56.

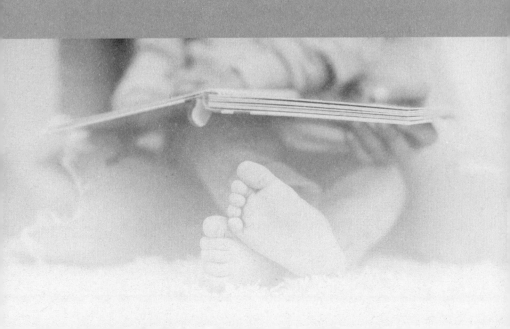

Part 2

Real-Life Strategies

3

Simplify with Scripts

Lisa

The morning started well...or at least it seemed to. I woke early, made coffee, and even showered and got dressed before my little ones were awake. Things were looking good.

After the kids had gotten up, I walked into the kitchen with my youngest son on my hip. My daughter stood leaning on the open refrigerator door, a scowl on her face. "There's nothing to eat," she said.

I looked at the overflowing refrigerator and suggested, "You can have eggs, yogurt, cereal and milk..."

She closed the door. "I don't like any of those."

Before I could figure out my response, a voice yelled down the stairs, "Mom, he has my book, and he won't give it back. He's going to cut it with scissors!"

I turned and ran up the stairs, my youngest son still on my hip—and so my day began.

Have you ever had a situation with your child go rapidly downhill, and you couldn't figure out how to regain control? I know I have. I try to remember what I've read, but in the stress of the moment, it all seems to slip away.

When our children from hard places joined our family, it seemed there was far too much to learn and implement in our home. Some days I felt I was drowning and barely making it through the day. I wondered, "How would Dr. Purvis handle this? What would she say?"

Likewise, a friend once wrote on a social media site, "Does anyone have a direct line to Dr. Purvis? I need to know what to say to my child." Let me share a few things I've learned from her.

Just a Few Words

Parenting children who have histories of harm requires us to learn many new skills. How do we connect in a difficult moment? How do we meet the need of our child's heart when our brains are casting about, trying to remember just what we are supposed to do? Where do we start?

I needed something simple to grab hold of, and thankfully I found this tool—I could simplify my life by using scripts to instruct my children.

To create a new family culture, you need a new language. Children from hard places are often on high alert and will not respond to a barrage of words; their brains simply cannot receive that much input. As Dr. Purvis will explain, when our children are upset, or "dysregulated," they are unable to process our words. Many of us tend to want to talk them through it, yet science tells us that this is not the way to go.

Scripts are short verbal cues used to redirect children toward optimal behavior. Scripts are quick phrases; they're simple and communicate clearly. Scripts can also help caregivers learn new ways of communicating with their children.

We need to limit our words to as few as possible. If you're a talker like I am, it is very difficult, but these short, simple phrases guide us and our children through the day. Russ and I even remind each other of this by saying, "Words," when we hear each other going on too long and piling words on top of words.

Let me give you a few examples from my family.

"Let me see your beautiful eyes."

Making eye contact is one of the first goals of attachment, but many of our children are not comfortable with this and will avoid it as much as possible. They may have learned as infants that eye contact was futile or even dangerous. They may also have sensory processing challenges that make eye contact uncomfortable. The eyes are a window into our children's hearts and minds, so we want to gently teach and encourage them to make eye contact.

Standing at the kitchen sink and calling instructions over our shoulders will not work. We need to stop our own hurried lives, move to our children, and look at them. Dr. Purvis uses the phrase "Let me see your beautiful eyes." It's amazing how effective this is for getting them to meet our eyes.

Sometimes I say "Look right here" as I tap my face between my eyebrows. They can't seem to resist looking up for a moment, and then I have an opportunity to reinforce their eye contact by smiling and saying "You have such beautiful eyes" before I move on to the instruction.

Some of my children have significant sensory processing challenges, which I'll discuss in a later chapter. Though they have been our children for many years, they still find eye contact difficult. I learned early on to set the bar low enough for them to succeed. I didn't expect sustained eye contact. Sometimes a fleeting glance is all I would get, and I needed to praise them for that: "Good job showing me your eyes!"

Even now that they are older, when I need to be sure they really understand me, I begin by getting eye contact. If they look away, I pause until they glance back at my face, and then I continue speaking. When I see their eyes, I know they are attending to what I'm saying.

"Listen and obey."

This is another great script. We may be inclined to say, "Now kids, I want you to listen because this is really important, and I expect you to obey me." Or worse yet, we may call out an instruction and then, when they don't obey, begin a discussion about how disappointed or frustrated or unhappy we are.

Some of our children don't have conscious memories of their parents. Others had parents who neglected them, so the concept of parents being in charge is new and strange. I recall an adopted child telling me it was easier at her orphanage because nobody paid attention to what she was doing. She didn't understand that having a mother to watch over her was a good thing; it only felt invasive and uncomfortable.

Using only three small words—"Listen and obey"—is much more effective. When I introduced this script, the kids weren't used to it yet, so I prefaced it by saying, "I'm going to give you an instruction. Get ready to listen and obey." Soon I was able to simply use the short script.

"Are you asking or telling?"

When a child says, "Give me a drink" or "I want a cookie," we direct them to ask rather than tell us what they want. We are saying to the child, "I'm listening to you and want to help you with what you need, but you need to use respectful words." A playful, "Are you asking or telling?" may be all they need to be reminded.

As my children become more familiar with the scripts, I begin to ask them to use complete sentences, so when they say, "Cookie, please," I teach them to say, "May I please have a cookie?" Initially, however, it's important to set the bar low enough that our children can be successful, so the goal should simply be that they ask rather than tell you what they need. In fact, if you are facing complex challenges, you may need to set this goal aside for now.

Just the other day, my son said, "When I come inside, give me my lunch."

I said, "Are you asking or telling?"

He replied, "I guess I was telling. Want me to try it again?" And he did: "When I come in from playing, can I please have lunch?"

It was easy to smile, give him a little hug, and say, "That was such nice asking."

"Would you like a compromise?"

When I heard this phrase for the first time, I thought, "Wait a minute—a compromise? My child is supposed to obey, not negotiate with me." But I soon embraced this powerful tool to help my children. Some of our children had learned that they had no voice and no power; they were victims of their life circumstances.

We want to teach our children that they *do* have a voice and that their thoughts and feelings matter to us. They need to know we will meet their needs. Two ways we can demonstrate this are by offering choices (which I'll discuss in a later chapter) and by allowing them to make compromises.

Here's an example. My son was playing with Legos while I made dinner. I was busy and trying to be efficient, so I said, "I need you to set the table." Honestly, I should have paused and realized he was engaged in his activity, but this is real life, and I didn't think of that in the moment.

His reaction was abrupt and disrespectful, and it could easily have become downright explosive. I immediately knew I had started off on the wrong foot, but how could I turn it around?

I held up my hand in a "stop" gesture and said, "Hold on, let me see your eyes." When he looked up, I said, "I see you were concentrating on your Legos, and you're not quite ready to stop. Would you like a compromise?"

He gave me a grumpy yes. That wasn't quite what I was hoping for, but it was respectful.

"Let me hear it," I said.

"Can I finish building this one thing and then set the table?"

"That's a good compromise. Dinner won't be ready for thirty minutes. Can you finish in fifteen minutes?"

"I think so."

"Okay, set the timer for fifteen minutes, and when it rings, I want you to hop up and set the table. Got it?"

"Got it."

We didn't end up in a standoff over setting the table. We reached a solution that was agreeable to both of us without a tantrum, yelling, or any of the other behaviors that so easily come with kids from hard places. There was no urgency in the task, so I was able to be flexible with my son. This allowed him to think through the process and find a good solution. Because I responded calmly, he was able to stay regulated and suggest a compromise.

"Use your words."

Using this with younger children may not be a new idea, but we often don't consider how important it is with much older children. We say "Use your words" to toddlers, but a ten-year-old from a hard place may have learned that nobody hears her words and that she needs to act aggressively or be out of control to get our attention.

When our young daughter joined our family, she was completely unaccustomed to being parented. The smallest thing would dysregulate her, leading to rages that lasted a long time. Teaching her to use words rather than behavior to express herself was an arduous task, and it is still ongoing. But it's a goal worth pursuing.

Here's an example. She came home from school and stormed in the front door, tossing her backpack and coat on the floor. She stomped into the kitchen with a scowl on her face. I greeted her warmly, but she ignored me, turning away toward the refrigerator.

I walked over to her and said, "Whoa...take a breath and tell me what's going on."

Still she didn't respond. I reached to put my hand on her shoulder, and she jumped back saying, "Don't touch me!"

"Okay, I won't touch you, but I need you to slow down and use your words."

She turned her back to me and crossed her arms. I waited and then calmly said, "Use your words, and tell me what you need."

"I'm hungry!"

"Okay, let me help you find a snack."

She turned toward me, opened the refrigerator, and let me help her. The situation could have become much more explosive, but this time, she was able to use her words to express her need, and I was able to meet it.

> "Use your words, and tell me what you need."

"Try that again with respect."

I seem to use this script nearly every day. We have an entire chapter devoted to the importance of teaching respect, so I'll save those stories for later, but respect is foundational to our parenting.

Dr. Purvis

As Lisa shared, using scripts is simply a way to create a vocabulary of family values. Scripts were one of the first tools we used in our early therapeutic summer camps, and we continue to teach professionals serving children from hard places and their families to use scripts. Before we talk more in depth about scripts, let's back up a bit and explore why the concept of scripts is so important, particularly for children who come from hard places of abuse, neglect, or other trauma.

Think about it this way: In the earliest days of life, a newborn often cries. In the best-case scenario, a loving adult responds consistently and attentively, and the child learns he is precious and valuable and that safe adults will attend to his cries and meet his needs. In fact, before an expectant mother gives birth, her body's senses—including her hearing—begin adapting to hear her child's voice. This phenomenon primes the mother to respond to her child's needs before he is even born.

Once baby arrives, his parents spend hours looking into his eyes, establishing a precedent of loving eye contact. Holding a baby, rocking him, gazing into his face, and other affectionate interactions release dopamine in both parent and child, which is a brain chemical associated with learning and joy. Through these repeated affectionate interactions, parents establish a child's capacity for a lifetime of trusting, meaningful relationships. As we've discussed in earlier chapters, every answered cry is a yes to a child's need for safety and connection, and it builds the child's understanding that there are trustworthy, loving adults on duty. Assuming this baby continues to receive warm, sensitive caregiving and does not experience any major traumas early in life, he very likely will grow up to become a child whose behaviors can be easily guided and mentored by the caregivers he trusts.

But what happens when a child *doesn't* experience consistent, warm, sensitive caregiving by a loving adult in early development? Remember that even prenatal harm can affect a child's development both inside and outside the womb. If an expectant mother is overly stressed, research shows that her elevated stress hormone levels can affect the baby's brain development. If a baby's mother abuses drugs or alcohol while pregnant, regions of the brain critical for communication may be radically altered.[1] And if a child did not receive warm, sensitive, consistent caregiving early in her life, or if she experienced abuse, neglect, or other trauma, her cries were probably not answered with yeses, and she will lack trust and connection with safe adults and will lose her voice.

Now that we understand the impact of early experiences on a child's voice, let's look at scripts through a lens of trauma. Children who experienced optimal early years of caregiving will likely have greater capacities to process many words, accept correction, and look to safe adults for guidance. Children who experienced adversity are more likely to have auditory processing challenges, exhibit aberrant behaviors, and distrust even the safest adults in their lives.

Scripts help alleviate these issues because they...

- are short and easy to understand,
- provide quick guidance and reminders for children (and caregivers!), and
- build safety and connection through shared language.

> Scripts provide a way for caregivers to communicate simply and for children to know their voice matters.

Short scripts are designed to guide children toward more optimal behavior through play and nurturing rather than punishment. The scripts are short and seem simple, but they carry great meaning and help families like Lisa's build a vocabulary that honors relationships and quickly reminds children of the skills they are learning. Most importantly, scripts provide a way for caregivers to communicate simply and for children to know their voice matters.

One of the most common questions we receive from caregivers is "Where can I get a list of the scripts?" There isn't a definitive list of scripts because every family and situation is different, and scripts should always be tailored to the culture and language of each family.

One example comes to mind from my work with a residential treatment facility in Texas that serves high-risk teens. The staff was implementing scripts in each cottage on campus, and a group of teenage boys took issue with the script "No hurts," which we borrowed from the Theraplay Institute and typically use with younger children.[2] This script wasn't quite resonating with these teenage boys. Their caregiver suggested they create an alternative to remind themselves not to fight physically or to use unkind words. The boys came up with "Be cool."

In her earlier examples, and later in this chapter, Lisa provides a great list of scripts to get you started. We've found some to be helpful over the years, and others are unique to her family. As you choose scripts for your own family, make sure each one helps meet the goals of building connections and giving voice. Here are a few more guiding principles to help you develop your own scripts.

Keep scripts short, clear, and concise.

Children from hard places may have trouble processing many words, particularly in a behavioral "crunch" time. Using fewer words helps children to process concepts quickly.

Practice scripts when everyone is calm and regulated.

Trying to teach a script to a child who is melting down is about as effective as trying to repair a leaking roof in a rainstorm. When your child playfully practices scripts during calm times, she will more likely be able to recall the script and process its meaning regardless of whether she is behaviorally regulated or dysregulated.

We recommend caregivers and children practice scripts by role-playing. Did you know we learn more quickly when we are having fun? Children get a kick out of practicing the "wrong way" first and then the right way. Here's a quick example.

Adult: Sweetie, it's time to pick up your toys and go to bed.

Child: No, I don't want to! (The more exaggerated and dramatic the child acts in the role play, the better!)

Adult: Oh, wow…that was great practicing *no* respect! Let's try it again *with* respect. Sweetie, it's time to pick up your toys and go to bed.

Child: Okay, Mom!

Adult: Woo-hoo! That was a great job of showing respect—high five!

Be sure to keep these times playful and light, always praising your child for a great job doing it the wrong way *and* the right way!

Use scripts as reminders, to correct behavior, and to praise good behavior.

Recognize the times your child presents the desired behavior—with or without the prompting of a script—and praise him genuinely and lavishly. This is called "marking the task." It helps your child identify the motor memory for communicating the right way, and it encourages him to adopt that behavior. Think of scripts as signposts for guiding a child toward their highest potential.

Deliver scripts with the appropriate tone.

By design, scripts are intended to replace excessive negative jargon, which can be demeaning and shaming. However, scripts must also be delivered with an appropriate tone for both the child and the situation. Remember, scripts are a reminder for positive behavior and not an admonishment for negative behavior.

You might find the scripts Lisa and I suggest don't ring true to your family's language and culture and may come off as inauthentic or condescending to the children in your care. This is precisely why we urge you to develop scripts personalized to your family. Use scripts to guide your child toward optimal behavior and the goal of connection. Using a warm, nonthreatening tone of voice and having a relaxed, open facial expression while delivering scripts will help you achieve these goals.

When a child feels safe and connected and the survival regions of the brain are calmed, the higher cortical regions for language and cognition are activated.[3] In a sense, by looking back in a child's development and meeting those basic, unmet needs for safety and connection, you can help the child grow and thrive in optimal ways. We have found that a consistent, nurturing environment over a sustained period is necessary for the child's brain to develop a mastery of their responses. The use of scripts is a wonderful baby step toward that amazing goal.

Lisa

I'll close this chapter with one last script I have used regularly over the years.

"Is this a big problem or a little problem?"

Some of my children have extreme reactions to disappointments, mild injuries, and parental correction. Vulnerable children may not be able to match the intensity of their responses to the intensity of the situation. They are on high alert and are ready for something big to happen.

A wise therapist taught my family to use our hands and say, "I can see this is really hard for you, and I want to help. Let's see if we can figure it out. Is this a big problem [hands held far apart with arms wide open] or a little problem [hand held close together]?"

If my child can't or won't respond, I might spread my hands apart again and simply say, "Big or little?"

Often my child can slow down and realize it is actually a small problem. Once their brain is engaged, we can find a solution together.

Key Takeaways

- Scripts create a vocabulary of family values.
- Scripts should be tailored to the culture and language of each family.
- Scripts should be short, clear, and concise.
- Scripts should be taught while everyone is calm and regulated.
- Tone is of the utmost importance when using scripts. A script delivered in a frustrated, punitive, or sarcastic tone will be ineffective and will not build connection.

Try It Today

Choose one new script and try it several times over the next few days. Here is a list of additional scripts to help you get started:

Scripts for Young Children

"Ask permission."

"Show respect."

"Be gentle and kind."

"Use your words."

"Listen and obey."

"Compromise."

"Let's have a redo."

"Match my voice." (This models volume control.)

"Make it right." (A prompt for forgiveness and restitution.)

"Stick together." (Group Theraplay recommends this to encourage listening and proximity.)

"No hurts." (Theraplay for Groups uses this for bodies and for feelings.)

Scripts for Older Children and Teens

"Be cool." (This replaces "No hurts" or "Gentle and kind.")

"Check with me." (This replaces "Ask permission.")

"Work it out" or "Let's make a deal." (This replaces "Compromise.")

"Hold up!" (This replaces "Try it again.")

"Think it through."

"Take a breath."

"Calm it down."

"Got it?"

4

Combat Chronic Fear

Lisa

Children from hard places commonly had unpredictable environments. Caregivers, even loving ones, may have changed unexpectedly, familiar smells and sounds disappeared with a move to a new home, recognizable voices were silenced. And those are best-case scenarios for many children with early adverse experiences. Other children experienced profound neglect, hunger, cold, fear, and abuse of many kinds.

Our children's brains are affected by these early experiences, and by the time they come to us, the more primitive areas of the brain (like the amygdala and other parts of the limbic system) are prone to taking over at the slightest threat. This means that when a child from a hard place feels threatened by hunger, a loud sound, or even a harsh tone of voice, the more advanced areas of the brain shut down and our child may resort to "fight, flight, or freeze" to cope.

> I've learned that my children require different things to feel safe in our family and home.

To help our children heal, we need to meet their needs in a way that makes them feel profoundly safe in their environment and with us.

Over time I've learned that my children require different things to feel safe in our family and home. They are all unique, with different histories and personalities.

There are, of course, many basic rules and routines that provide safety for everyone:

- No one uses violence—kicking, hitting, spitting, biting, and so on.
- Everyone respects Mom, Dad, and each other.
- Everybody has a place in the family as well as responsibilities.
- As a family of faith, we honor God in the way we treat each other.

In addition, each of my six youngest children needs certain things to feel safe and loved in our family.

Helping Each Child Feel Safe

One of my daughters feels safest when she can express her needs and knows that we hear her and will meet her needs. She is the middle child of eleven and holds a unique place in our family, standing between two different groups—the oldest five and the youngest five. It's easy to get lost in the middle. When four children from hard places joined our family, she was not heard, and her needs were not met. It breaks my heart to admit that. Thankfully, we became aware of this, and we are making efforts to hear her and meet her heart's needs by carving out time in our days to listen to her and assure her she matters. One-on-one time allows a perfect opportunity for this, but it's hard to come by in a big family. Although a lunch date would be great, running an errand together is more realistic most days.

Another daughter feels safest when she is near me. The more time she has with me, the better. She thrives on affection, comforting touch, and hugs. When she was young, being held in the rocking chair filled her heart. She is also sensitive to the tone of my voice and does best when my tone is very warm and calm. She is a teenager and will tell you her love language is quality time. She's absolutely right.

Another daughter feels safest when the refrigerator is full and she can make choices about what to eat—as long as there aren't too many choices and the options are all things she likes. Sometimes we have cooking days. I help her fix and freeze several breakfasts for herself. School is hard work for her, so she feels safest when I am attentive to her homework and help her be organized and prepared. She craves routine and structure and is least happy when the day is relaxed and unstructured. This makes weekends and vacations difficult, and we've learned to plan carefully, even providing alternate activities for her.

One of my younger sons feels safest when Russ and I are close by. He can play independently, but he also likes to check in with us. He does not like surprises and is easily upset by loud sounds or sudden, rough movements. He does not like unexpected hugs or touch but is getting better at coming close and letting me hug him. He also thrives when there is a consistent bedtime routine, which includes Russ reading to him, praying with him, singing, and tucking him in each night.

My youngest daughter feels safest when she is certain we will protect her from being bullied or hurt. She is our daughter by birth, and she also needs to feel safe and secure. Her world was shattered when our new children joined the family. We have worked diligently to restore her sense of safety. There were many months when I just couldn't hear her amid the din, so I try very hard to listen to her fears and concerns.

One of my young sons is very secure and rarely feels worried or unsafe...unless there is turmoil with one of the other children. As the baby of our large family, he is quite adored and gets lots of positive attention. He is securely attached not only to Russ and me but also to his older siblings, so he is easily comforted and calmed.

Sleep

Sleep is very important for children, but many children with histories of harm experienced fear, discomfort, or abuse at night in their previous homes. They have trouble sleeping because they are watching out for danger.

One of our children had traumatic nightmares, and another was so hypervigilant that she was unable to sleep through the night for many months—or maybe it was years; my sleep-deprived memories are foggy. She often slept next to me or in a sleeping bag by our bed. Giving our children a safe and cozy spot to sleep lowers their anxiety and hypervigilance.

One of our sons has always preferred sleeping in small, confined spaces. Rather than on his bed, he often chose to sleep in a sleeping bag tucked between a chair and a cabinet. One day Russ dug out the kids' old play tent and asked our son if he wanted to put his sleeping bag inside. He loved it and seemed to relax in the cozy enclosure with his favorite fleece blanket, teddy bear, and stuffed puppy. In his tent, our son felt safe and slept in peace. That was several years ago, but even now, he will occasionally ask for his tent, and we're happy to get it out again.

Choices

Me:	You can have your snack at the counter or at the table—those are your two good choices.
My son:	But I want to have bad choices.

This incident reminds me how consistently I still use the technique of offering two choices and use my hands to physically demonstrate them to my child. This small tool has been so effective for us not only in reducing stress over decisions but also in giving our children a measure of control in their lives and reducing their anxieties.

When possible, I present my children with two options, touching one palm as I offer the first choice, then the other as I offer the second choice. Then I hold out both palms, indicating that my child needs to choose between the two options.

"Would you like to do a puzzle [touching one palm] or play with Legos [touching the other palm]?"

When my daughter hesitates, as my more traumatized children are likely to do, I use even fewer words: "Puzzle [touch one palm] or Legos [touch the other palm]?" This technique encourages my child to make a choice rather than argue, debate, or refuse to choose. It is both visual and physical, and she will generally respond by touching or pointing to the hand with the option she has chosen.

Another similar method is holding up two fingers and then lightly touching one finger and then the other when presenting the options, as Dr. Purvis does. Both methods demonstrate to the child that she has choices.

Here is an example of what I might do if one of my children is having a hard time getting along with her siblings:

"You aren't able to play happily this morning. Would you like to [touch one palm] sit at the kitchen counter and chew a piece of gum, or [touch the other palm] rock in the rocking chair with me?"

She rarely makes a quick choice, so I may repeat (even more simply), "Gum or rock?" as I touch each hand.

At that point she will almost always point to one of my hands. I praise her for making a good choice, and then I follow through. I have offered two appropriate options, and she gets to choose which one to accept, which increases her sense of safety.

If for some reason my child is unable to make a choice or refuses to choose, I might say something like, "Are you asking for a compromise? If you are, you need to ask with respect." Whether we offer a compromise or choices, we are working toward the same goal—to disarm fear and build trust by providing practical evidence that the child has a voice and that safe adults will listen.

Food

Many children from hard places have suffered food deprivation. Each of our adopted children experienced this, but for one of my daughters in particular, the effect has been profound. Issues about food—what to eat, when to eat, how much to eat—require a dispro-portionate amount of time and energy and are a significant drain on the loving relationship I want with her.

A simple food plan makes life easier for both of us. For several months, she had chicken and rice for breakfast every single morning. We cooked a large batch together, and she froze it in individual serv-ings. This made our morning routine significantly better. Lunch was one of two choices each day. We stored beef jerky in her backpack for a snack at recess. Her afternoon snack was either hummus or tuna. Can you tell my daughter craves protein, particularly meat?

The most challenging meal of all has always been dinner because she has to eat what I have prepared. To this day, dinnertime is difficult. I try to include at least one item I know she will eat, and for a long time, rice was always an option. Now, as a preteen, she is learning to accept the food I prepare and make choices without outward turmoil.

Dr. Purvis

We all know the importance of ensuring a child's safety. Even first-time parents or new caregivers consider the safety features of baby gear and toys. We teach very young children about the dangers of hot cooking surfaces, moving cars, swimming pools, and strangers. These measures are often enough to let the typically developing child know that safe adults will protect him from potential danger.

If you have welcomed a child from a hard place into your home, it's likely you have taken many additional measures to ensure your child's physical safety. *You* may know your child is safe, but have you considered whether *he or she* feels safe?

Children who have experienced trauma often live in a state of chronic fear long after the threat of real danger has passed. We often hear caregivers say, "But my child doesn't act like he's afraid." Children may not show typical signs of fear, but many have been afraid so long that they don't even recognize the dark gnawing of their unspent fear.

Brain Development

To understand the effects of chronic fear on the brain, we need a basic understanding of the brain's structure and development. If we think of the brain as a multistory house under construction, the "downstairs" part of the brain is genetically wired in place at birth, allowing a child to breathe, eat, sleep, and hear. Survival functions are rooted here.

At this point, very few connections in the "upper floors" are formed. These more sophisticated parts of the brain govern higher functions: complex thought, reasoning, emotional processing, memory, speech, and the ability to regulate behavior. This circuitry develops and becomes hardwired in the brain only through time and repeated experience.

When a child experiences trauma, such as abuse or neglect, it can skew the wiring of the brain as well as its structure and chemistry. The lower, more primitive, survival part of the brain can become overdeveloped from reacting to fear, while the critical upper floors may be underdeveloped and suffer. Trauma triggers the lower part of the brain and shifts it into overdrive, where it creates a chronic state of fear and produces toxic stress.

> What may look like sadness, anger, or even mental illness is often the manifestation of chronic fear.

If we look at these children's neurochemistry levels, we find high levels of cortisol, the body's stress hormone. Parents are often surprised to discover that what they considered aggressive and combative behavior is really driven by fear. Other parents are surprised to find that their child's withdrawn and whining behavior is driven by fear as well. What may look like sadness, anger, or even mental illness is often the manifestation of chronic fear. Hidden beneath this child's behavioral repertoire is a desperate, unmet need to feel safe.

Think back once again to the early days in a newborn's life. The repeated cycle of the infant expressing a need and the adult meeting the need establishes a pattern of felt safety and trust. This is what John Bowlby, founder of attachment theory, describes as a "secure base"—an attentive, loving adult who meets a child's needs consistently over time and becomes the child's anchor. As the child grows and begins to explore independence, the child knows he can return to his secure base when he feels afraid. Out of this relationship, this "dance" between child and caregiver, the child learns what it is to be human: He is safe, he finds joy in relationships, and he can trust.[1]

Children who did not experience the attentive, compassionate care of a secure base may appear independent, a trait all parents hope to instill in their children as they grow into adolescence and adulthood. But as we discussed in chapter 1, a child's dependence on a safe adult is developmentally appropriate. A child who appears independent without a secure base does not trust safe adults to comfort them in distress. It's important to remember that true, healthy independence grows out being dependent earlier in life.

The Long-Lasting Effects of Trauma

Without intervention, relational traumas—such as the loss of parents, a natural or man-made disaster, or abuse—can have lasting impacts even years later. One study showed that children adopted from hard places had elevated levels of cortisol six and a half years after they had been adopted from harsh or neglectful environments.[2]

In fact, a single episode of trauma can cause alterations in the chemicals associated with fear. For example, researchers conducted brain studies on adults who were in New York City on September 11, 2001. More than three years following that single traumatic day, adults' brains registered significantly higher levels of activity in the regions for fight, flight, or freeze.[3]

It may seem obvious that trauma affects a child's behavior and

sense of felt safety, but what about children who have not experienced trauma in the traditional sense? Parents often ask us what could
be driving the confusing behaviors they see in their children who
have been in their home since birth, whether biological, fostered, or
adopted. These parents are often surprised to learn that a difficult
pregnancy or a difficult birth can affect a baby's stress system.[4] Tiffany
Field's studies of neurotransmitter levels among pregnant mothers
and newborns documented a strong connection between the events
that occurred during pregnancy and the child's neurochemistry after
birth, including the level of fear hormones.[5] In essence, an expectant mother's stress levels during a difficult or stressful pregnancy can
impact her infant's brain.

Evidence of Healing

Science tells us that trauma—even prenatal trauma—often
severely impacts a child's ability to feel safe and connected. While
research predicts a sobering trajectory for these children, there is also
hopeful, research-based evidence of healing. In the same way that a
single trauma can affect brain development, we have found that in
an attentive, nurturing environment, cortisol levels can be reduced.[6]

I love how Lisa gives examples of what makes each of her children feel safe. By understanding our children's histories, discovering their unique needs, and consistently meeting those needs, we can
change their brain chemistries. In the same way the mother of a typically developing newborn responds to her baby's cries for hunger by
providing milk, Lisa meets one daughter's needs for food by keeping
the refrigerator full and involving her daughter in meal and snack
preparation. Meeting the needs of a newborn certainly looks different from meeting the needs of a preteen, but both infant and adolescent experience safety and connection when their caregiver responds
attentively and consistently.

I'll share one example of the importance of disarming fear. In a therapeutic summer camp in the late 1990s, we discovered that even though the children were physically safe in their adoptive homes, they did not feel safe. Our early data demonstrated that children who had been adopted many years earlier still had twice the level of cortisol that would be expected of a child in a safe, loving home.

In our first cortisol study, we obtained salivary markers for cortisol the week before camp and found that the level was twice that of optimal levels. Two days into the first week of camp, we took saliva samples to measure cortisol again and found that the levels were every bit as high as they had been in the home. The following week, as the children began to feel safe and less fearful, we discovered that their cortisol levels had fallen into the normal range, where they remained through the rest of camp.[7]

Predictability

Researchers (and many parents!) have known for years that optimal development is most often established in predictable environments where children have an appropriate level of control. Children from hard places often lack these experiences, so we must find creative, intentional ways to make predictability and appropriate levels of control part of a child's daily experience.

Predictability simply means "I know what is coming next." Whether we ourselves have come from hard places or not, most adults like to know what to expect. Imagine how scary it must be for a child with a lifetime of unpredictable experiences to trust adults—even adults who love them.

Recently, one of my young grandsons needed stitches in his forehead. While the doctor was setting up his tools, he said "I'm going to numb this area so you won't feel the stitches, and this part will hurt a little." The doctor continued, "When I start putting in the medicine to numb it, I want you to count with me, starting at six and counting backward to one." The painful numbing procedure could not be avoided, but this creative emergency room doctor made the experience predictable by letting my grandson know what would happen and by counting with him. Instead of crying and pulling away, this eight-year-old was calm and cooperative, knowing that after they counted down to one, the hurting part would be finished!

Control

Control is the second part in this pair of fear busters. Children are empowered when they know they have a voice that will be heard and that they will not be acted upon against their will (as they may have been in previous environments). In the story of the clever emergency room doctor, the plan to count backward also gave my grandson a sense of control and allayed his fears.

Lisa's example of giving choices to her son is a great way for caregivers to appropriately share power with children, which enhances felt safety. Giving choices provides a concrete way for caregivers to guide youngsters toward appropriate decisions and build their autonomy while helping them feel safe. This does not mean children are in charge; rather, they become collaborators in creating the outcomes in their lives. We call this "shared power."

Fear is a primal emotion and is controlled by the more primitive brain structures. Lectures, scolding, and punishment do not help—in fact, they create even more fear. Fear must be calmed through connection and nurturing before we address specific behaviors. Our hope is that the tools described in this chapter will give you practical and effective ways to create connection by giving your child a voice and disarming fear.

Lisa

Just in case I'm giving the impression that I'm anything but a flawed mother, here is a little story for you.

It was a hectic morning. Piles of dirty clothes crowded my laundry room, and breakfast dishes filled the countertops. I breathed deeply and moved quickly from one task to another while also finding a Band-Aid, getting drinks, and wiping up a spill—and that was before even getting started on my to-do list, which seemed a mile long. I felt a bit harried.

The kitchen began to look better, the washer and dryer were running, it was almost time for me to tackle my list—and then the little boys asked for one...more...thing. I heard myself saying much too loudly, "I will get you a snack, but do not ask me for one more thing!"

My teen son glanced up from the computer, and I felt a twinge of shame. It was not pretty, and even as I was saying it, I knew I should stop, slow down, breathe, and speak calmly.

My little boys froze, looking at me with wide open eyes. Then one of them jerked away from the counter and crossed his arms over his chest. I was chastened by his response. I went to him and gently touched his arm, but he pulled away. I knelt and held out my arms to him. I told him I was sorry for shouting and asked him to forgive me.

He fell into my arms, saying, "You scared me!"

My heart clenched. I'm the mommy; I'm the one who is supposed to be healing his broken, scared heart.

Then, through his tears, he said, "You...broke...my...heart."

Now my heart, too, was broken.

Though that morning may have been tough, I know that I need to calm myself to heal my child's heart and use a voice that communicates love. If I just can't get it together, I need to take a moment to pray, breathe, and calm myself, even if it means locking myself in the bathroom for five minutes.

We spent a little bit of extra time snuggling on the sofa while reading stories before naps that day. I gave the boys extra hugs and kisses. Thankfully, amazingly, my little boys love me despite my faults.

Key Takeaways

- Even if a parent knows their child is safe, the child must feel safe.
- Fear can often look like aggressive or combative behavior in children.
- Predictability and appropriate levels of control promote felt safety.

Try It Today

Spend time reflecting on what makes each of your children feel safe. Think of ways you can meet these unique needs and build feelings of safety in your family and home.

5

Nurture to Heal

Lisa

Children who have experienced trauma, neglect, and other difficult life circumstances come to us with wounds we can't see. One of the most important means of connecting and facilitating healing is through the gift of nurture.

If I could own one tool for promoting attachment and encouraging connection, it would be a rocking chair. Rocking my children is possibly the most important thing I do to nurture them. Over the past thirty-two years, I have spent hours rocking children in my wooden rocker, in my glider rocker, and in an old hand-me-down rocking chair. Some of these chairs haven't matched my decor, but they've been the perfect place to rock my little ones (and even bigger children) on a hard day.

One morning our daughter cried for an hour over a perceived injustice in the division of chores. She would not eat breakfast or talk to me; she only cried and repeated over and over, "Me *two* chores, my sister only *one.*"

Finally I coaxed her into the rocker and wrapped my arms around her. As we rocked, I whispered in her ear all the calming words that came to my mind. I told her I loved her. I told her I knew it was hard learning to live in a family, because things aren't always fair. I told her there were warm pancakes waiting for her when she felt better. Her crying quieted, and her arms wrapped around my neck. She pulled my face down to hers and whispered, "I love you, Mom."

We held each other close and rocked our sorrows away. The simple rhythmic, repetitive movement was calming for both of us, and it still is as we seek to connect in the hard moments.

Time-In

As parents of vulnerable children, we must learn new ways to deal with difficult behaviors. Many parents have been taught that when our children are being disrespectful or disobedient, we should give them a time-out. In direct contrast, Dr. Purvis teaches us to use "time-in" and keep our children close.

Let's be honest—when our kids are challenging, we want a break! The last thing we want is to have them sit close by. But in this, as in so many aspects of parenting, our children must come first. Sending our kids away does not help them to learn or to connect with us.

When one of my children is struggling, I have them sit in a big stuffed rocking chair next to the kitchen, where they can be close to me. This is the "think it over" spot. As soon as they are calm and ready to talk, they say "Ready, Mom," and I am right there.

Time-in is also useful with older children. A few years ago we were having a tough time with one of our adopted children. One day after school, she came to apologize for something that had happened that morning. I hugged her and forgave her. Then she said, "But I know I'm going to have a consequence." I explained that there would be one but that it might be a little different than she expected. Rather than a punishment, we would keep her physically close to us for a time. Our hope was that limiting contact with peers and even siblings would reduce her dependence on them and build her trust in us.

I'm not saying this didn't feel like a punishment to her; it did. She wasn't thrilled with the idea of being next to Mom and Dad rather than off playing with her sisters or spending time with friends. Before joining our family, she had developed the necessary skill of taking care of herself. Now she needed to learn to trust us and to know we were in charge of the family.

We've learned that keeping a struggling child close is essential. This ensures that they aren't able to go off with the other kids out of our line of vision, which is when disrespectful talk, grumbling about parents, and other destructive things can happen. A couple of nights ago, this meant one child going to bed in our room, another in her own, and the last one doing homework downstairs until the other two were asleep.

> We've learned that keeping a struggling child close is essential.

This is similar to time-in, but it can last for a number of days, depending on how well our child accepts our support and allows herself to be parented. Time with trusted adults is helpful, whereas time with peers (even siblings) may not be. This means I have to come up with things we can do side by side. We've had fun cooking, tackling a decluttering or cleaning project, shopping, and just sticking together.

One of our daughters and I still laugh about the day I had her keep one finger hooked through a belt loop on my jeans. At first she wasn't happy, but as we moved about the kitchen, it became increasingly humorous. She enjoyed the closeness even if she didn't want to admit it.

Eye Contact

Eye contact is also important for nurturing and connecting with our children. When we give them kind and gentle eyes, we meet a deep need in their hearts. Think of the way adults gaze at a baby: We coo at them and make noises to get them to look at us. We mirror their expressions and marvel at how cute they are. This is part of the normal attachment process many of our children did not experience. Thankfully, we can begin today to give them this healing gift.

One school day, amid the morning madness, I walked into the kitchen, where I saw Russ instinctively modeling one of the simple skills drilled into us as we've worked to build trust and attachment. Our daughter was sitting on a stool at the counter, and Russ had gotten down low in front of her to gain eye contact. At first she refused to look at him, but then she glanced up. As he spoke softly to her, she looked in his eyes.

As they connected on this deep level, Russ touched her cheek; she smiled and hugged him. This simple tool reached her when words alone could not.

Another tool to encourage eye contact is a gentle chin prompt—touching the child lightly under their chin or, in the case of a child who is not ready for touch, just holding your hand under their chin without touching.

> Giving eye contact conveys how much you value your child, and requesting eye contact is a way to gain a child's attention should you need to communicate an important message. Never use eye contact as an excuse to give your child a mean and angry stare; instead use your eyes to communicate in a loving and nurturing way. The goal here is to be healing. Give your child the experience he would have received if he had been with you from the beginning, when you could have cradled him in your arms and gazed at him with love.[1]

Dr. Purvis

When children come to us with histories of harm, they often behave in confusing or even hurtful ways and may have difficulty developing deep, meaningful relationships with others because of their wounds. When parents reach out to our institute because of their children's behavior, I always try to remind the parent of what their child lost—the care, the tender love, the eye contact, and the touch of a parent. So in every instance, even in moments when behavior might need correcting, nurturing connection must come first. I continue to ask you to look at your child through the lens of their history—not to excuse bad behavior, but to help you become attuned to your child's needs and to see behavior as an expressed need. The goal is to ask yourself this question when your child is misbehaving: "What does my child need right now? What is this behavior saying?" Clearly we must deal with behavior, but a child who is acting out behaviorally needs both structure *and* nurture to grow, thrive, and learn to trust the safe adults who love them.

As we've discussed in previous chapters, during early development, attaching and connecting is the main job of the first year for a parent and child. The parent spends endless hours holding the child, touching her, looking into her eyes, and whispering words of love and comfort to her. If your child missed these experiences, there are many ways you can re-create this nurturing environment, even if your child comes to you when they are older.

> Clearly we must deal with behavior, but a child who is acting out behaviorally needs both structure and nurture to grow, thrive, and learn to trust the safe adults who love them.

Lisa's example of her family's rocking chair is a wonderful way to provide nurture to children. The rocking not only meets an attachment need but also provides vestibular sensory input—that is, the motion gives children the sensation of a change in position. Many children from hard places have a vestibular deficit. In an orphanage environment, they may not have been picked up often, for example. Or in an unsafe home, perhaps their cries were not met by a loving caregiver. While rocking is an excellent way to spend time nurturing your child, there are many other ways we can infuse nurture into everyday interactions with our children, including when we correct their behavior.

Eye Contact

I love to lower myself into a child's field of vision. There's a wonderful thing that happens when our eyes are at the same level as our little ones'. Establish the habit of getting on your child's level to show your full attention and care. Eye contact not only forges deep connection but also sparks remarkable brain reactions, increasing dopamine, which promotes learning. In fact, a study from the University of Cambridge found that eye contact between infants and adults syncs their brain waves, which is key to communication and learning. If children did not have the early experience of eye contact with loving adults, helping them learn this important skill is crucial.

Many children from hard places may be averse to eye contact. For some children, it's fear of abuse or of being seen. For others, it's shame or sensory overload. With your child's history in mind, work to establish eye contact as they can tolerate it. Start slowly by glancing at your child briefly and then looking away, increasing sustained eye contact as they begin to feel safer. Start the habit of asking your child, "Could I see your beautiful eyes?" and following with praise: "Wow, I love those great eyes!"

Many children respond well to playful attempts for eye contact. If I have a child who struggles to make eye contact, I might say something silly, like "Let's see...are those eyes orange? I can't remember!" Usually this will prompt the child to look at me, and I'll say, "Oh, that's right. They're beautiful blue! I love to see those eyes." Slowly, over time, we can increase the amount of eye contact our child is willing to give. Eye contact should never be forced but should come organically as our children learn to trust us.

With eye contact comes deeper trust and connection. Working on this simple yet important skill improves brain chemistry, regulation, and most importantly, your relationship with your child.

Balancing Structure and Nurture

One of the biggest questions I get from parents and caregivers is, "When do I use structure, and when do I use nurture?" When addressing behavior, I often use the analogy of walking, with one foot for structure and one foot for nurture. Ideally, we walk equally with both feet. Most of us, however, tend to be more adept at using one "foot" over the other. Leading with the structure foot while dragging the nurture foot behind will harm a child's ability to trust; conversely, leading with the nurture foot while the structure foot limps along will harm a child's ability to grow and mature. Getting the right balance of structure and nurture is the most common challenge I see in caregivers. With practice, it is possible to interact with your child with the healing mix of structure and nurture.

So what will this look like practically? It may seem counterintuitive, but keeping a struggling child close to you is an important step in healing trauma. This principle should guide the way we look at misbehavior and our responses to it. Simply put, children who are struggling due to histories of harm need to be mentored in regulation *and* relationships, as both set the foundation for behavior. Bringing a child close provides the safety of proximity with a loving adult and the nurturing aspects of a relationship. Our goal is to mentor a child's brain so he or she can be successful, and that can be done only in the context of a safe relationship.

Lisa touched on time-in versus time-out. When I send a child to time-out, in essence I'm saying, "Go away until you can be good." When I sit with or near my child during time-in, I'm saying, "Buddy, I see you're having a hard time, and I'm right here to help you."

Feeding Connection

In chapter 2, we talked briefly about Jude Cassidy's work and the four skills of meaningful relationships.[2] Children who have experienced adversity often struggle to create deep, meaningful connections because they lack the ability to give care, to receive care, to know their autonomous selves, and to negotiate their needs. As we intentionally nurture our children, we can look for ways to model, teach, and practice these skills.

In her next section, Lisa gives an example of feeding her young daughter in a moment of emotional distress. The practice of feeding is a powerful way to strengthen the bond between child and caregiver, which informs all human relationships. Here's how feeding encourages the development of each skill:

- *Give care.* The parent offers food to the child, feeding them gently and asking the child what color or flavor they would like.
- *Receive care.* The child accepts the food from the parent.
- *Practice autonomy.* The child can forego care by using respectful words.
- *Negotiate needs.* The parent asks for the child's permission before giving care and honors the child's decision.

Since feeding is typically reserved for young children and babies, it can be difficult to think of a way to incorporate this practice that doesn't feel patronizing or embarrassing to older children. Here are a few ideas to get you started:

- Make a game of tossing popcorn into each other's mouths.
- Take turns offering each other a novel color-changing candy, such as gobstoppers.
- Use a toothpick or a straw to feed each other gummies.
- Order two dishes to share at a restaurant and pass bites to each other.

Caring for Hurts

Offering care when the child is hurt is another practice we often use to create opportunities to nurture. I've had many adoptive mothers confess to me that even though they hate to see their child hurting or sick, they relish the opportunity to meet their physical needs and nurture their bond. If your child approaches you with a hurt, even one that may seem small or dramatized, celebrate the fact that she came to you with her need! Gently rubbing ointment on a sore or applying a bandage to a wound is powerful—even more so when it's followed with a sincere "Sweetheart, I'm so sorry you got hurt. I hope it feels better soon."

Rather than waiting for your child to get hurt or feel sick, incorporate the practice of caring for "hurts" on a regular basis. In TBRI nurture groups, we set aside a time for passing around Band-Aids and sharing our inside and outside hurts. The interaction usually goes something like this:

- Everyone in the group is given a Band-Aid (or stickers or lotion).
- Form groups of two. Person 1 asks if he or she may put a Band-Aid on person 2.
- If person 2 says yes, person 1 asks if the hurt is on the inside or the outside and listens for a response.

  o Person 1 then asks, "Would you like to tell me about your hurt?" and listens with empathy.
  o Person 1 then asks where person 2 would like the Band-Aid. Person 1 applies the Band-Aid gently and says, "I'm so sorry you're hurt."

- If person 2 says no, person 1 respects the answer and offers the Band-Aid to save for later or for person 2 to apply themselves.
- Repeat the process, reversing the roles.

Here is how this exercise can promote the four skills for meaningful relationships:

- *Give care*. Provide a Band-Aid and a safe touch to another person and listen to their hurts.
- *Receive care*. Share personal hurts and receive a Band-Aid from a safe person.
- *Practice autonomy*. Request to forego care with respectful words, and respect another person's request to pass.
- *Negotiate needs*. Choose a Band-Aid, ask for a pass, or compromise.

This can easily be adapted for family life or in a residential care setting. Perhaps once or twice a week, your family can talk about hurts and exchange Band-Aids before bedtime.

Infusing nurture into your daily interactions with your child will not only strengthen your connection but also help them enjoy future meaningful relationships.

Lisa

It's difficult to remain nurturing when life gets busy and our schedules are too full. Special events, vacations, and holidays can be especially challenging.

The Christmas our daughter was eight still holds a place in my memory. We were enjoying the fun and frenzy of Christmas morning. She was happy, but as the day progressed, I felt I was watching her inch toward the edge of a cliff. At first it wasn't too noticeable. She was a little irritable and jumpy, shouting out what her siblings' gifts were as they were opening them. This heightened the tension in the room, making us all a little edgy. Her smile was too big, her eyes were too bright, her voice was too loud...She was on high alert.

Once the gifts were opened, I focused on preparing the dinner we would enjoy later that day. But Russ and I continually needed to calm things down, diffuse situations, and navigate disagreements. Our girl was edging closer to the edge of a meltdown. I saw it, but I was busy and thought I could prevent her from falling apart. I told myself I would get to her in *just a minute.*

I was wrong.

I tried to calm her, but I was too late. She was completely dysregulated—screaming, hitting, and crying. I hadn't kept her close enough. I had been too busy to keep my own child safe. She had our attention now. Russ and I scrambled to think of the therapeutic tools we knew.

We tried a few, but she couldn't hear us. She was in an all-out state of fear, and although we knew she was completely safe, she was overwhelmed with a sense that her life was in danger.

Finally, with a bowl of some of her favorite potatoes, I pulled her onto my lap in the big rocking chair and fed her one bite at a time.

As she slowly ate, I whispered comforting words into her ear, like I would to a baby. "Come here, little love. Take a bite...I know you're hungry. This will taste good...I love you. It's going to be okay. You'll feel better in a moment."

I kissed her wet cheeks.

She said nothing, but she opened her mouth each time I offered the spoon.

Her body relaxed against mine. She sighed. I rocked her back and forth in my arms.

We rested, and when she was calm, we returned to the kitchen. We smiled, and Russ lifted her in his arms, hugging her close.

Then we carried the rest of the food to the table, called the family together, and had Christmas dinner—where she had three more servings.

Key Takeaways

- Misbehavior is the expression of an unmet need.
- If a child needs nurture and I give him structure, I harm his ability to trust me. If a child needs structure and I give him nurture, I harm his ability to grow. Nurture and structure must be used hand in hand.

Try It Today

Think about a simple way you could incorporate nurture into your daily interactions with your child. Choose one from the following list or create one of your own.

- Rock together in a rocking chair.
- Read aloud to your child.
- Promote eye contact by getting down on your child's level to talk with him.
- Play a feeding game with your child, putting a treat into their mouth and having them put one in yours.
- Take even small injuries seriously by offering compassion and a Band-Aid.
- Take a walk together. Hold hands if your child is comfortable with touch.
- Give your child a hand massage.
- Help your older child or teen choose a fuzzy blanket of their own at the store.
- Play a game of your child's choice.
- Sing songs to your child or with her.

- Do fingerplays with your young child. (You can find many online.)
- Use familiar connecting phrases, such as "I love you to the moon and back" or "I'm so glad I'm your mom."
- Create bedtime routines, including prayer.
- Have one-on-one time.
- Share hugs.
- Use nicknames.
- Offer special food treats.
- Share inside jokes.
- Tuck notes in backpacks or stick Post-its on the bathroom mirror.
- Sit still and listen to your child with your full attention.

6

Teach Respect

Lisa

Most children learn respect from the time they are tiny. They learn that their parents are in charge, will keep them safe, and are worthy of respect. A child from a hard place may have learned that adults cannot be counted on, are not safe, and are certainly not worthy of respect. Now this child has you for his or her parent, and respect is not coming naturally. So how do we teach respect whether the child is six, ten, or sixteen?

One morning when our son was six, he thrust his glass at me and said, "Milk!" This would have been cause for praise if he were a little one learning to talk, but at six, he could certainly do better than that. Rather than launching into a long lecture about that not being a respectful way to ask for something he wanted, I smiled and said in a light tone, "Try that again with respect."

He lowered his glass and said, "Mommy, may I please have more milk?"

I answered, "Sure! Great job asking with respect!"

He smiled, clearly pleased he had done a good job.

That ended quite nicely, but many of our interactions do not. If this conversation had come to a stalemate, or if a control battle was clearly beginning, I might have offered choices as compromises. Sometimes we must set the bar low and then move it up as a child is able to regulate his emotions and actions.

Hands down, the tool I use most frequently is the simple script, "Try that again with respect." Then I stop talking and wait. Often my child will rephrase their request in a way that shows respect.

In *The Connected Child*, Dr. Purvis addresses this in no uncertain terms.

> Any time a child demands something or asks for it disrespectfully (this includes screaming at you), that request must be denied. Period. For example, let's say your son comes running and belligerently shouts at you, "Give me money for the ice-cream truck!"
>
> Don't get distracted by his urgency. Calmly say to him, "If you want something, you need to ask with respect. If you ask without respect, the answer will always be no."[1]

For many families, this is simply common sense, but when we're parenting children from hard places, it can be difficult to know what is most important to tackle. Respect must be at the top of the list.

Respect—Step-by-Step

Let me show you step-by-step how I would handle this on a good day with one of my children. Suppose my son has just commanded me to help him with his chore.

I start by saying lightly, "Let's try that again with respect."

If he crosses his arms, furrows his brow, and continues being disrespectful, I move to the next step. I move closer and get down to his eye level. I touch his cheek and say, "Respect with your face." I touch his arms and say, "Respect with your body." I touch my lips (or his) and say, "Respect with your words."

I give him a moment to process, and then I might touch his cheek, arm, and lips again without using words. Remember, we are almost always inclined to use too many words, and dysregulated kids can't process them.

If the disrespect continues, I will likely tell him to sit in the "think it over" spot (or if necessary, pick him up and carry him), which is typically the big chair near the kitchen. I tell him that when he is ready to make things right with me, he needs to say, "Ready, Mom," and I'll be right there to talk with him and help him.

If I'm being a really phenomenal parent, once he has settled down and is ready to be respectful, I give him a redo by returning to the original spot and having him ask me again with respect. Sometimes I manage to do this, but other times we move on because I have lots of kids and life keeps moving. I simply don't take the time I should. Still, a redo is powerful. If you are in a time of intense training, make it a priority.

And If That Doesn't Work...

Obviously, I'm giving an example that hasn't led to a tantrum, which takes things to a different level altogether. If your child is volatile and reactive to touch, *do not touch him* when you get down to his level. Due to their history, children from hard places may perceive this as a threat and will likely push you, slap at you, or run. None of these are the reactions we want when we are teaching respect. Give the child a bit of space, and use gestures for teaching respect without touching the child.

In that case, I get down on his level and draw a circle in the air at the level of the child's face while saying "Respect with your face." I draw my hands downward and say "Respect with your body." I touch my own lips and say "Respect with your words."

Scripts, like the ones we mentioned in chapter 3, are very helpful in training children, and we use lots of them. Otherwise we are tempted to launch into long explanations using far too many words. Kids can only process so many words, and when they are dysregulated, that number drops dramatically.

When all else fails, your child may simply be tired, hungry, or unable to work it through with you. If he will allow you to rock him or read a story and tuck him in for a nap, go with it. A glass of milk or small protein snack might help him calm down as well. I've been known to give my kids a spoonful of peanut butter, a sippy cup of milk, or a cheese stick as they sit in the "think it over" chair. Children who come to us with very challenging histories need firm boundaries but also lots of grace. We may need to say, "I can see you have some big feelings about this. Let's take a break and talk about it in a few minutes."

> You may have to set the bar low at first to give your child some initial success.

I know this can be ridiculously tiring and frustrating. So many days I find myself wondering how to handle something and lacking confidence that I'm heading in the right direction. Besides, it is incredibly fatiguing to parent at this level, and more often than I would like to admit, I fail. There are days when I fall short of the ideal, and I need to take a short break, regroup, and try again. A few minutes in the "think it over" spot may help me and my child calm down enough to keep going.

Also, remember you may have to set the bar low at first to give your child some initial success. You may even try noticing when your child is doing a small thing well and say something as simple as, "Good for you, no crossed arms! You showed respect to Mommy."

With an older child who is being disrespectful, we move toward a "when/then" scenario. For example, "When you can make that request with respect, then I will take you to the swimming pool." It's not "*If* you can make it with respect," it's "*When*," because we want our children to know we believe they are capable of being respectful.

If a child is not yet able to be respectful at home, she isn't likely to be respectful in other environments, which means her world needs to be small. For my older children from hard places, this has meant going to school and church and spending time with one or two carefully chosen adults rather than peers.

Dr. Purvis

We all long to be treated with respect. For most of us, showing respect was an integral part of our upbringing. Showing respect—especially to adults—was expected and highly valued. To be treated with disrespect, especially by our children, can feel particularly hurtful and confusing. After all, showing respect to a loving adult shouldn't be that hard for a child, should it?

By now you may have guessed what I'm going to ask you to do next—to think back once again to early brain development. I return to this paradigm again and again because it is critical for caregivers to view their children through this lens to best meet their needs. By doing so, we are in essence *showing respect* for children's histories. Before we expect our children to show us respect, we must respect their needs.

Learning in Stages

A child who experiences optimal development learns the value of respect by example. Adults model respectful behavior by being attuned to their children and meeting their needs. After all, few people would expect a newborn baby to stop crying on his own without being fed, changed, held, or rocked. Nor would most caregivers interpret an infant's cry as a sign of disrespect but rather as an expressed need. We've talked about how this dance of meeting needs over time builds trust, felt safety, and the foundation for self-regulation. It also informs our understanding of how relationships work.

As children grow older, caregivers teach respect more intentionally. As children learn language, we teach them to add "please" and "thank you" to their first requests. As they become more mobile and start toddling toward the family cat, we might remind them, "Be gentle!" We teach them to pet the kitty in the right direction, touching it gently and kindly. We teach them to stop touching the kitty when it pulls away. Everyday scenarios like these can become the classroom for teaching relationship skills that were largely absent in children's hard places.

Respect is a higher-order process that is naturally accessible to children who have lived in loving and nurturing homes. But let's remember that no child is perfect, and even typically developing children with attentive, compassionate caregivers can sometimes struggle as they learn to show respect. For a child who lacked nurturing care, respect can be more difficult to master. Keep in mind that chronic fear limits access to the higher-functioning regions of the brain. A child who has experienced harm without intervention is often simply unable to learn to show respect until she feels safe.

> We cannot expect our children to learn respect until they feel safe and connected.

Caregivers may think a child's age is indicative of her ability to behave appropriately and show respect. For any child who has experienced harm, biological age will tell little about her ability to show respect. In chapter 1, we saw that children who have been fostered or adopted from traumatic backgrounds can have developmental ages that are half or less than half of their biological ages.[2] The stunning truth is that children with histories of harm are often only 40 to 50 percent of their chronological age in terms of developmental maturity. This underscores the importance of respecting our children's histories before asking them to master showing respect to others. We cannot expect our children to learn respect until they feel safe and connected. But research shows that when we create a safe place to begin to mentor, we quickly quiet the limbic system and activate higher cortical functions, facilitating the ability to show respect.[3]

In the home from which your child came, perhaps his words were not heard. For example, he may have cried out for his needs to be met, but his cry was ignored. Or he might have cried out for an abuser to stop harming him, but he was harmed even more. Disrespect was a way of life and a means of survival. Without the felt safety that is established from consistently met needs, it is simply unrealistic to expect a child to show respect without being compassionately taught and mentored. Though our scripts include only a few words, they convey this message to our children: "I'm listening to your words and want to honor your voice, but you need to ask with respect."

Looking at our children's behavior through the lens of their trauma allows us to see their behavior as an unmet need and gives us the opportunity to meet that need joyfully and consistently. As we learn to respect our children and their histories, they will feel safe, heard, precious, and valued, allowing them to learn and demonstrate the respect we desire as parents.

Lisa

One evening a couple of years ago, we had beef stir-fry for dinner, and our daughter remembered some fortune cookies tucked away in the pantry. Purchased for a special dinner a few weeks before, we had forgotten to serve them, so they added a surprise to the night's otherwise basic dinner.

We had fun reading the fortunes aloud and commenting on how appropriate (or not) they were to the recipient. Our youngest got one about long-term goals that we hoped might have something to do with completing potty training. Best of all was another child's fortune: "Your respect for others will be your ticket to success."

I couldn't have said it better myself. In fact, several times each day I say, "Let's try that again with respect."

The right words may come out of her mouth—but the tone tells me what is happening in her heart. We try again. Sometimes it goes well, other times we don't quite make our goal.

Russ and I are working hard to teach our children to be respectful. It is a tough battle, but the victories will benefit them for the rest of their lives.

Key Takeaways

- Respect is a higher-order process that is naturally accessible to children who have lived in loving and nurturing homes. For children who have experienced adversity and/or trauma, this process will not develop without mentoring.

- We cannot expect our children to show respect until they feel safe and connected.

Try It Today

Find time during your week to teach the concept of showing respect. Practice with your child during a calm, connected time, and then say, "Let's try that again with respect" when the occasion calls for it.

Recognize Your Child's Sensory Needs

Lisa

I love to greet my children in the morning as they come down the stairs and into the kitchen. This morning it went something like this when my daughter entered the room:

"Good morning. May I give you a hug?" I ask.

She approaches me sideways and leans into me, arms at her sides, while I hug her.

"May I have a kiss?"

She offers me her cheek, and I kiss her.

"Now can you give me a kiss?"

She laughs nervously and then kisses her hand and puts it on my cheek.

"How about a real kiss?"

She leans in, puts her hand on my cheek, and kisses her hand. She pulls back and laughs.

I smile. "That was the silliest kiss ever!"

She rests against me ever so briefly, and I give her a quick hug.

My daughter was quite young when she joined our family, and I assumed affection would come quickly. I couldn't figure out why she pulled away from hugs, resisted our touch, and struggled with eye contact. We feared it was an attachment problem.

Then our adoption therapist observed our interactions and asked some questions that began to add pieces to the puzzle. Our child showed many of the behaviors typical of sensory issues. Children with sensory issues are often too loud and too rough, moving like bulls in a china shop. They may make repetitive nonsense noises and rock themselves to go to sleep. Like my daughter, they often can't get enough of activities like jumping on the trampoline and swimming for hours and hours.

That was the beginning of our exploration into sensory process-ing disorder (SPD). With the help of an occupational therapist, we learned that children with SPD crave some sensations and are averse to others. We learned that deep pressure rather than light touch feels good to some children. Chewing bubble gum can be calming, jump-ing on a trampoline can help kids regulate, and a weighted blanket can help kids sleep. We gave up on the small things, like wearing socks, and focused on the big things, like taking breaks during school and getting enough time outdoors.

"Match My Voice"

Small tips made big differences. For example, my daughter talks loudly—I mean *really* loudly. She has no sense of her volume or what it should be. I used to say "Use a quieter voice" or "You're being too loud." The concept of an inside voice was beyond her. Then I watched a therapist working with her and saying, "Match my voice." My daughter didn't do it very well at first, but she is learning. That phrase seemed to click with her. Now she can often bring her voice down to a nearly normal range.

Not too bad for three small words.

Another fun way to teach a child to speak at a proper volume is with the help of a voice recording on your phone or computer. We make it a game, taking turns speaking at different volumes—soft, medium, and loud. Then we listen to our voices and note the dif-ferences. Normally we hear our voices internally, through our bones.

But when we hear our voices on a recording, we hear them externally, through the air. Hearing their speech out loud allows our kids to detect the sound of their voices more accurately.

Can you imagine the silliness potential of doing this with your child? You can sing, make funny sounds, or even read a book aloud together, making up voices for the characters. Most of all, we want to help our children become more sensory aware.

"I Got Scared"

My friend Amy shared this story about her son, Ian. When Ian was six, he went to vacation Bible school for the first time. She thought it would be a fun summer activity, and it was—but it was also a learning experience about SPD.

When she arrived to pick up her children at the end of the first day, the director took her aside to relate this story. During the closing activities, Ian and a new friend had gotten a little rowdy and were jostling each other while doing motions to the songs. Eventually Ian pushed the other boy, who fell and hit his head on the pew, getting a small cut.

Amy knew this was going to be a big deal for Ian to process and wanted to get him home quickly. The director suggested that Amy might want to take Ian to see the boy before they left and tell him he was sorry, but Amy explained it probably wouldn't go well and that she would talk with him at home.

As they left the church, Ian looked sullen and angry. He refused to make eye contact and grumbled that he was never going back. Amy's daughter began yelling that Ian had pushed the boy. Amy held her hand up to her daughter (a visual cue) and simply said, "Stop." She told all the kids that she would talk with their brother at home and that she didn't need any more information from them at the moment.

They arrived home, and as the kids piled out, Ian ran around the car to her door, and all his anger melted into tears. Amy gently touched under his chin to prompt eye contact and said, "I'm listening to you. Tell me what happened." He tearfully explained that he and the boy had been bumping into each other and playing when the boy grabbed his arm, and "...I got scared."

For a child with sensory issues, physical contact can seem threatening instead of playful. Ian has a hard time interpreting what different kinds of touch mean, so having his arm grabbed put him on high alert, and he shoved the boy away.

This made sense to Amy—she could see the scene unfolding in her mind. Amy assured him that she understood he had been frightened and that he didn't mean to hurt the boy. He cried on. She told him they would find a way to make it right with the other child, and Ian could tell him he was sorry he had caused him to fall. Ian was still resistant, telling his mom he was never going back to vacation Bible school. Amy assured Ian that he could stay home if he preferred but that he needed to ride along in the morning and decide after he was there.

The next morning, her sweet boy chose a treat for his friend (a small bag of Cheetos) and attached a note that Amy had written for him and he had signed. It read, "Dear Matthew, I am sorry I shoved you. I got scared when you grabbed my arm. I hope we have fun today."

Once they were at the church, he got caught up in the activities and decided to stay. Ian was eager to give his friend the present and seemed content. Amy talked to the director and told her a little bit about her son's sensory issues and that he has a hard time interpreting things.

Dr. Purvis teaches that children with sensory challenges should always be at the front or the back of a line, where they are less likely to be bumped and pushed. They may become aggressive or overreact when normal play and jostling occur—simply put, they just don't interpret physical contact well.

This was the first time Amy's son was in an environment where she could see him being labeled as a "problem," and it broke her heart. She told me, "Ian is definitely rough and tumble, but not mean. He is a sensory seeker in many ways and likes to move his body. He jumps on the trampoline, swings, rides his bike, rides the bouncy horse, chews bubble gum, sleeps with his weighted blanket, and generally needs a bit of help regulating. Understanding, and being able to explain sensory processing disorder, is very helpful."

Calming Space

Like Ian, my children need a lot of space to feel calm. Last summer we took a family vacation, and it reminded me of the importance of being aware of their sensory needs. One of the things I love about vacation is being together as a family, and frankly, we were together a whole lot.

Several of my children were getting tense and arguing with each other. They were very quickly frustrated and needed help staying regulated and calm. Then we had two days of rain, and it was a bit more than they could bear.

One of my little ones had an outburst that caught me by surprise, although in hindsight (which doesn't feel particularly helpful), I could have preempted the entire thing if I had been more perceptive. As the rain (and tears) came down, I asked him, "Do you want to go for a walk?" He did, so I dug through a duffel bag and pulled out our raincoats.

Then I remembered a sweet thing. The day before, we had gone to our favorite thrift store, where I'd found a darling pair of ladybug rain boots—in my size. I bought them thinking I would use them to run to the mailbox in the fall. But I needed them sooner, and here they were. The memory still makes me smile.

We headed out in the rain, and in a short time, my grumpy boy was calmer. We walked slowly down the hill, watching the water flow, carrying leaves with it and then spilling over the edges of an overflowing drain. We made our way to the side of the hill covered with blackberries, where we picked the plump ones and popped them in our mouths. He even let me put a berry in his mouth, although it took a few tries.

As we headed back to the house, he held my hand for just a moment, and my heart swelled. Understanding my son's sensory needs and gaining tools to help him have given us confidence as his parents. The challenges are significant at times, but we know we can help our son, and that is very rewarding.

Dr. Purvis

Sensory Processing in Everyday Life

Almost everyone can remember a room that was too noisy or rowdy, a smell that was too pungent or overpowering, or a touch that was unnerving. Each of us has occasionally wanted a little less light or less volume from the television. But for a child who has sensory processing disorder, these annoyances greatly interfere with everyday life, making it very difficult to adjust to the environment, process information, develop healthy attachments, and regulate behavior.

Current research shows that about one in every twenty American schoolchildren has SPD.[1] However, a much higher percentage of children coming from hard places may be reactive to some sensory experiences. These mystifying behaviors cause great angst for parents who don't recognize that their children's behaviors reflect changes in their brains from their early histories of neglect, abuse, or trauma.

The Impact on Early Development and Attachment

You may be surprised to learn how sensory processing problems affect the attachment relationship. Exploring and meeting a child's sensory needs can greatly benefit the relational bond between child and caregiver. In fact, meeting sensory needs and meeting relational needs go hand in hand.

By now you know that our early experiences inform our relationships. These same experiences also set the foundation for our ability to process sensory input. In optimal development, a caregiver responds warmly and consistently to a baby's cries and picks the baby up to soothe them. Beyond meeting the emotional need, however, the caregiver is also unknowingly laying the foundation for the sensory system. In this example, picking up a baby and holding her causes the fluid in her inner ear to move. This affects an important component of the internal senses—the vestibular system, which processes spatial awareness. The vestibular system is considered the "powerhouse" of our internal senses. A failure in vestibular functions often causes challenges downstream for the other senses as well.

Research gives us insight into the close relationship between the attachment cycle and the ability to process senses. Not surprisingly, children who appear to have behavioral or attachment problems often have high levels of sensory processing problems as well. In some of our earlier research, my team noted that an exceptional percentage of the children in our therapeutic summer camps exhibited signs of sensory deficits. Parents reported fewer positive attachment behaviors for children who had sensory deficits at the beginning of camp. But after several weeks in a sensory-rich and attachment-rich environment, children made breathtaking gains in behavior, cognition, and attachment.[2]

> Meeting your child's sensory needs is vital to his or her ability to feel safe, process information, and thrive in healthy relationships.

When we were intentional about meeting campers' physical needs, they felt safe to connect with and trust their caregivers. After the camp, parents reported that children exhibited many new skills, such as greater self-awareness of their thoughts and actions, increased desire for closeness and proximity, better eye contact, more displays of spontaneous affection, advancements in vocabulary, an increase in empathy, and a better capacity for following directions. As you can see, meeting your child's sensory needs is vital to his or her ability to feel safe, process information, and thrive in healthy relationships.

Behavior and Regulation

Sensory processing problems can often result in behaviors that seem mystifying. Lisa's example of a child's experience at vacation Bible school is a perfect illustration. Two boys were playing together, learning a new song and hand motions, when suddenly things took a bad turn and someone got hurt. To a person who is not informed about the effects of trauma, this episode could look like roughhousing gone wrong—or worse, bullying. But what we have observed over decades of research tells us otherwise. In our programs, children who had the most struggles behaviorally also had sensory deficits; specifically, tactile deficits. Unable to process the meaning of certain types of touch—even safe, appropriate touch—these youngsters often acted out behaviorally in response to a sensory aversion.

Sadly, there is a compounding set of behavioral and emotional costs for children who experience sensory challenges. They often have self-esteem struggles because they know they're not like the other children. Their social competency may be lacking because they can't understand other children's social cues. In the story Lisa shared, Ian did not understand the meaning of someone's touch, and his amygdala—the fear center of the brain—took over.

Some of the most striking research illustrating the impact of sensory deficits on behavior examined the behavior of primates. Landmark studies by Harry Harlow, his colleague Stephen Suomi, and others in the early 1970s documented dramatic alterations in the brains of young rhesus monkeys raised without nurturing care. In those studies, scientists noted changes to the cerebellum of young primates raised in neglectful or abusive circumstances. The cerebellum, located at the back and bottom of the brain, is named for the Latin word "little brain" because it plays such an important role in motor control. It is also believed to influence cognition, attention, and language and to regulate responses to fear and pleasure.

Harlow and his team discovered greatly reduced levels of synaptic connections, which correlated to a monkey's confusion about sensory messages such as touch, taste, smell, sight, and sound. Most sensory messages are processed first through the thalamus and then sent to the appropriate part of the brain for processing. Of the five types of messages, only smell goes directly to the amygdala, where it is processed immediately. The amygdala "decides" whether the scent signals danger, and that helps determine the subject's response.

Similarly, children who have experienced early abuse, neglect, or trauma may also have reduced levels of synaptic connections, making it difficult to interpret sensory input. The pungent-smelling lunch of a classmate may be an annoyance for children without sensory challenges, but for many previously harmed or neglected children, the overwhelming smell may mistakenly alert danger. Numerous times, I have been called in for a parent-teacher conference to defend the aggressive reaction of a child who sat next to a peer who was opening, for example, a tuna fish sandwich.

Understanding Children's Responses

Without intervention, children with sensory processing challenges respond to too much sensory input in three ways: fight, flight, or freeze. And these reactions are common for children who have a traumatic history. Knowing this, it's important for caregivers to begin understanding these children's behaviors as survival strategies rather than acts of willful disobedience. Melting down, running away, withdrawing, or becoming whiny is often the only thing a sensory-overloaded child can do. These are the only tools they have to cope with an onslaught of sensory input if they don't have support from caregivers who understand the effects of trauma.

Perhaps you have a similar story from a child in your care. Think back to the last time your child had a behavioral meltdown or an episode. What led up to the event? Could it be possible that the episode was triggered by a sensory issue?

Here are just a few examples of ordinary activities that could trigger a fear response from a child with sensory challenges:

At School

- transitions (too much chaos in the hallways)
- art class (touch aversion to Play-Doh or finger painting)
- music class (overwhelming noise or movement)
- PE class (overwhelmingly noisy and chaotic environment, and touch aversion to games like tag or capture the flag)

At Home

- visits to the grocery store (overwhelming smells or noises)
- shower or bath time (touch aversion to water sensation or temperature)
- mealtimes (overwhelming scents, tastes, and textures)
- bedtime (touch aversions to being held, being rocked, or physical affection)

Proactive Strategies

As you can see, daily life for a child with SPD can be extremely difficult. Fortunately, many proactive tools are available to help our children cope.

Proactive strategies for informed caregivers may include a variety of tools, which will vary by child and situation. Remember that every child is unique. Families will greatly benefit from consulting a trauma-informed occupational therapist to assess any sensory processing challenges and help make a plan to cope.

Considering what we know from research, one of the best pieces of advice I can give to parents is to spend a great deal of time just watching your child. What do they seek? What do they avoid? What textures do they like and dislike? What are their behaviors, and could there be a possible connection to a sensory issue? Keep a journal of your child's behavior so you can find a pattern in their actions. This record is also beneficial if you decide to consult a therapist.

Many families we have met have found help from the use of weighted blankets, weighted bears, weighted neck rolls, and other weighted tools. Like an infant snuggling in the arms of a loving adult when they are crying, weighted items create a sense of safety and calm. Using weighted objects releases calming neurotransmitters, and research shows us a relationship between these neurotransmitters and sensory issues.[3]

Based on what you observe in your child's behavior, another proactive strategy is to teach the child strategies for self-calming when their senses might get overloaded. It's important to practice the strategies during calm times, so they can access them in times when they are triggered. Just as Amy helped her son process the incident at vacation Bible school, you can sit with your child when they are calm and help them explore where they have challenges. Try asking questions to help your child identify his or her triggers and become self-aware without shame. Here are a few examples of questions you could ask:

- "Sweetie, it seems like you have a hard time at school when your class is in the hallway on the way to lunch or PE. Is it too loud for you in the hallway?"

- "I wonder if art class is hard for you because sometimes it feels funny to work with clay or finger paints. What do you think?"

- "Was it scary when your friend accidentally bumped you in the lunch line? Maybe we could ask your teacher if you could be at the front or the back of the line so you don't accidentally get bumped."

Remember, you are your child's advocate, not their adversary. By helping them identify their sensory triggers, you also empower them to cope with other challenges they may encounter.

Here are some good coping techniques that may help:

- Let your child choose a high-quality essential oil (dilute it per the directions) and teach them how to use the scent to calm themselves.

- Teach your child key phrases to help them ask for what they need.

    1. "It is too loud in here for my ears. May I play in the other room for a while?"

    2. "The Play-Doh activity is 'icky' for me. May I do a different activity?"

- Encourage your child to use a "fidget," such as a fidget spinner or a stress ball, to provide sensory input in stressful situations.

- Use weighted items to help calm your child. Always be sure to follow the guidelines for weight and let your child be in control of putting the items on or taking them off their body.

Informed and compassionate parents can make tremendous strides in guiding their children to use their words and not their behaviors to tell adults what they need.

Lisa

Prior to understanding SPD and connected parenting, an incident like Amy's vacation Bible school experience would have been very embarrassing for me. My own pride would have gotten the best of me, and I probably would have corrected my son, adding a twinge of shame: "You know you can't be so rough. I've told you this before, but maybe you just aren't a big enough boy for vacation Bible school." Can you see it play out? I likely would have been more concerned with parenting in a way that seemed right to the other parents than connecting with my son and correcting him in a way that would teach him something.

When I first heard of SPD, I was so consumed with learning about trauma and attachment that I chose not to delve into sensory challenges. I remember feeling that I couldn't possibly learn about one more thing, read one more book, or manage one more appointment, but I am so glad we did. The best gift we received was a new understanding of our children's behaviors. What looked like attachment issues or aggression was often a response to sensory challenges. Having sensory-aware eyes helped us tremendously! Meeting our kids' needs requires some creativity and thought, but it is fun because when it works, we get a big payoff.

> What looked like attachment issues or aggression was often a response to sensory challenges.

Several years ago, I said good night to my daughter, and she let me kiss her on the cheek. As I turned to leave the room, I saw her use the back of her hand to wipe the kiss away. Part of my mommy-heart felt sad that she didn't want my kiss, but I wondered if there were other things going on. Calmly I asked, "Can you tell me why you wiped your cheek?"

"It felt wet."

There you have it: Sometimes it really is that simple.

Key Takeaways

- Children from hard places often have difficulty interpreting sensory input.

- Meeting a child's sensory needs is vital to his or her ability to feel safe, process information, and thrive in healthy relationships.

- Consider the possibility that perceived attachment problems may be prompted by sensory preferences or aversions.

Try It Today

Be curious about your child's sensory preferences and then partner with your child to choose a coping strategy from this list—or come up with your own!

- Try a weighted blanket or item.
- Explore scents that are calming.
- Utilize fidget toys to help regulate.
- Teach key phrases for identifying sensory needs.

8

Adapt Your Strategies for Teens

Lisa

Teens are some of my favorite people. They're figuring out who they are and making plans for their futures. But what if a preteen or teen joins your family through adoption or foster care? Can you parent them using the same tools we've discussed in the previous chapters?

Yes—and no. We must adapt the concepts to fit these kids' developmental stages.

Quite a few of our family's friends have adopted older kids and teens. Many of these children suffered loss and multiple tragedies and spent years in orphanages. Some of them dreamed of having a family one day, especially when they saw babies and little ones being adopted by families from other countries. They had lots of ideas of what it might be like to live in America, where everyone was rich and lived in a big house—at least, that's how it seemed in the movies they watched. An internationally adopted teen told me he thought Americans threw their dishes away after eating rather than washing them. He also thought everyone had a pool in their yard.

One family adopted a boy who had always dreamed of being an only child and especially wanted to be adopted by a professional athlete. The family that adopted him had five kids and lived on a farm in Nebraska. This was not what he'd imagined. He wanted a dad who would play catch in the backyard and then drive the family convertible to get ice-cream sundaes. In contrast, his dad spent most days on a tractor in the fields.

Nobody asked this boy what he wanted. Life in an orphanage had many challenges, but it was the life he knew. Now he'd been torn from his friends, language, and culture and set down in a big family in Nebraska. They thought he would feel loved, but it took a long time for that to happen.

A few years ago, a teen joined our family for a respite weekend through foster care and stayed with us for two and a half years. Foster care is full of surprises. Once again, we added a youth to our family who had experienced an entire life before meeting us, and although our foster daughter and the boy in Nebraska have very different histories, there are also similarities.

This brings me to one of my most important points: Older youth and teens must be given a voice. They have opinions and have managed their lives for years without us. Their experiences and opinions should not be tossed aside.

Many youth from hard places have found remarkable ways to survive. These skills may not be necessary anymore, but they don't just fall away. Children who have experienced deprivation often look at life with scarcity in mind, as if there is still not enough to go around—not enough food, clothing, attention, or love.

Meeting Teens' Needs

Because they may not trust us yet, older youth will revert to what they know to create safety for themselves. Our goal is to be flexible so we can meet their needs. When we give them a voice, we build trust and feelings of safety simply by listening.

As with younger children, we can build this trust with preteens and teens by providing for their needs and asking their preferences. If food scarcity was an issue—which is quite likely—give your son or daughter a box with snacks they've chosen, and put a fruit bowl on the counter. If nighttime abuse was common, perhaps a loft bed would make him or her feel safer.

Attachment in the traditional sense is a beautiful goal, but it may not always be possible with teens, especially if they are only with you for a short time. Attachment is built by meeting our children's needs hundreds and thousands of times. Older youth can meet many of their basic needs on their own. They are in the natural process of separating from parents and caregivers.

The goal with teens is building trust and connection. I want to be a safe base for my kids, the one they turn to when they need support and help. I want to meet their needs—both the practical and the emotional.

As with younger children, we need to keep our own histories and triggers in mind. What were your teen years like? Do *you* have wounds you need to process? This may be a good time to talk through your adolescence with a good friend or professional counselor.

When I feel myself being triggered, my best strategy is to step away for a moment and take some slow, deep breaths. Sometimes that means going in the laundry room to collect myself or texting a friend to ask for support.

Scripts are still useful with older youth, but they need to be adapted to show respect for their age. I might not say "Ask permission" to a teen, but I might say "Check in with me." In our family we say "Calm it down" when energy is ramping up. I also say "Listen up" when I need a group of my kids to pay attention.

Don't be surprised if older youth and teens have specific sensory needs. The good news is that it's fun to figure out how to meet these needs together. I have a son who shoots hoops endlessly because it is calming and he loves basketball. Another one of my kids wears ear protection headphones in the morning when noise really bothers him. Several of my kids, including a few of my teenagers, have weighted blankets to promote sleep. Gum and fidget toys help youth stay calm in the classroom (request permission from the school if they aren't typically allowed).

One of our daughters asked for a weighted blanket and a sound machine for her seventeenth birthday. It was a joy to go to the fabric store as she chose special fabrics for her blanket, and she loves how well it helps her sleep.

Other Opportunities to Nurture

Keep your eyes open for opportunities to nurture older youth. One of the best times to meet their physical needs is when they're injured or sick. Kids who normally won't tolerate being comforted may be more open to it when they're resting on the sofa feeling miserable. Asking what sounds good to eat and giving medication (if necessary) show you care. Keeping their water bottle or mug of warm tea filled demonstrates that you're paying attention.

One of my sons rarely gets sick, but not long ago he stayed home from school, feeling weak and achy. This gave me a unique opportunity to nurture him by fixing requested foods, giving him medication, and providing fresh water and comfy blankets. Best of all, we watched shows he chose (all related to sports) while sitting on the sofa together. This is a teen who generally is very independent and doesn't like physical closeness. It was a moment I chose not to miss.

Other opportunities to nurture older youth include driving them to appointments, staying near when they have hard meetings (especially foster youth), and teaching them life skills, like setting up a bank account. The most thrilling support may be sitting, slightly terrified, in the passenger seat as they practice driving. Parenting teens requires courage!

Respect

Older youth will not automatically give us their respect simply because we are their new parents. We must earn it, but we must also not allow overt disrespect. This may require honest conversations like this: "Having parents is new to you, and I know it might feel strange to have a mom. I will always do my best to treat you with respect, and I need you to speak to me with respect too."

I use scripts like "Try that again with respect," although I often shorten it to "Try that again." "Are you asking or telling?" is useful with older youth, especially when said with a smile. I seem to use it often with one of my kids.

> The worst parenting I've ever done has been when I've parented out of fear.

Parenting older youth and teens from hard places is a true adventure. We may need to be more flexible than we've been with our other kids. It's also important not to be caught up in fear. The worst parenting I've ever done has been when I've parented out of fear.

Dr. Purvis

Sometimes parents are disheartened when they first learn about trust-based parenting, saying, "Well, my child is a teenager. Is it too late?" If that's you, let me give you this encouragement. In many respects, working with a teenager can be optimal. They often have more cognitive capacity than a younger child, so their ability to partner with the parent is greater. You can bring an adolescent under your wing and be their companion in ways that you can't with a younger child, and you may be able to relate to them in ways that you couldn't with a younger child.

We have worked with very high-risk adolescents and used the same techniques to build trust that we used with toddlers. Obviously, asking for eye contact from a teen looks different from asking for eye contact with a little one. When we nurture a teen, we use a different tone than when we nurture a five-year-old. Instead of saying "You're so precious" or "How did you get to be so cute?" I will say, "Wow, you're a great kid. I love to be with you."

Instead of stroking the head or touching the cheek (as I would with a younger child), I might put my hand on or just near the shoulder of a teenager, using either symbolic touch or actual touch.

> At every stage of development, we use the same interventions with the goal of creating the same holistic environment.

At every stage of development, we use the same interventions with the goal of creating the same holistic environment. And we've had magnificent results with teenagers in this holistic environment with insightful and compassionate caregivers.

We do three things in every environment where we serve high-risk children and adolescents:

- We meet physical needs with food, water, and sensory input.
- We meet connection needs by putting the relationship at the focus of every interaction.
- We correct behavior and thinking by disarming fear, allowing the authentic child beneath to emerge.

The most important thing I do when I first meet a teen or preteen is to observe them. What do they like? What makes them recoil? What sensory things do they seek? What sensory things do they avoid? What tastes do they like? Do their pupils dilate when I stand close to them? Are they afraid of me at some level? My observations inform every future interaction I have with this young person. Only when I am mindful and pay attention to the teen's needs can I begin to meet those needs.

Just as we would with a newborn infant, we can build trust by taking every opportunity to meet the needs of an adolescent. Allowing your teen to select their favorite snacks to keep on hand will help them feel safe knowing that food is available. Helping an adolescent select music that is calming to them will give them a strategy to use when they feel dysregulated. Lisa gives a beautiful example of going with her daughter to select fabrics for a weighted blanket to meet her sensory needs.

At a time in their lives when they are discovering who they are and who they'd like to be, helping teens notice what makes their bodies feel calm and regulated is a powerful relationship builder and teaches skills they can use for life. They don't need to be rocked and cradled, but teens still need to know their needs matter and that safe adults will help them meet their needs in appropriate ways.

Little Kids in Big Bodies

In my many years of working with children and teens from hard places, I've found that older kids often want to play like little kids. Adolescents are, in many ways, like little children wanting desperately to be loved, cared for, and nurtured. In fact, at one of our TBRI summer camps for teens, a group of fifteen- and sixteen-year-old girls approached me at the end of the day and asked for coloring books and crayons. They spent many hours over the next several days coloring together and with their mentors.

I share this story in hopes that you won't discount a child's chronological age and think that they are too old for certain activities. With a teenager, you will need to be careful to respect their developmental age, their cognitive and social/emotional capacities, their chronological age, and the peer pressure to appear like a "normal" teen. Let your teenager lead you in the things they like, and then guide them with appropriate boundaries.

One of the most heartbreaking situations I see is when parents say, "Well, he's fourteen years old. He's too big to be scared at night."

Please don't make that mistake! If he's scared at night, celebrate that need and meet it. Some parents will say, "He just wants attention." May I gently remind you that needing attention means your child or teen has a need for connection? I ask parents to reframe "He needs attention" as "He needs my care." Oftentimes parents realize that their child may not have the skills to ask for their needs to be met in appropriate ways. Maybe when they ask for attention they're annoying or noisy, but if you can reframe an attention-seeking teen as one who needs care, you can make great gains in mentoring your adolescent as they learn new skills.

Shared Power

One of the delightful things about working with teens and young adults is that they love to learn how to share power. Some would argue that a three-year-old also loves to learn to share power—and they do! But a teen has the cognitive capacity, reasoning, and logic to partner with caring adults in ways that young children do not.

The idea of sharing power makes some caregivers uneasy. I hear very often from parents and other caregivers, "If I share power and give him a choice or a compromise, I'll lose my power!" But this is what I would say to that fear: If you share power with this child or adolescent, you prove it belongs to you and it is yours to share.

If nobody consistently comes to meet the needs of children with histories of trauma, they stop using their voices. Instead, they use aggression, violence, manipulation, triangulation, and control to get their needs met. Those are survival systems for a child without a voice. But when we share power with appropriate boundaries, we give these children voice and build felt safety. When children and teens feel safe, they know they can use words to get their needs met and can lay aside the maladaptive strategies they've used before. Sharing power is one of the most trust-building things an adult can do with any teenager.

Model Disclosure

Another powerful way to connect with your teen is to model disclosure. By sharing our own previous struggles or challenges with our teens, we help them know they aren't alone. I've often told the youths I serve about my own history of abuse as a young child. I purposely choose this hard piece of my history because I know it can resonate with their own stories. I want them to know that I understand that part of their world, their fear, their pain, and their distrust of adults. If you're a parent or a caregiver and you want to learn to be a healing force in the life of the teen that you love or serve, it is critical that you level the playing ground and model trust and connection. Our children will never heal until they find their voices, which we can help give them by setting an example with our own disclosures.

When choosing what to confide to your teen, it's critical to share your experience with no expectation that the child or teen will feel responsible for your pain. Choose something age appropriate that will not make the child or teen feel as if they need to apologize, sympathize, or meet *your* need in some way. Remember, the goal of this exercise is to forge connection and create a safe space for teens to tell their own stories. One of my favorite things about teens is that they can sniff out disingenuity and phoniness—or authenticity—in an instant. Even if you have not experienced anything like what your teen has suffered, you can share honestly from your own experiences, recognizing that your stories are different.

Seeing the Need

Many people look at typical teen behavior and see rebellion, disrespect, and defiance. Sure, there may be some of that while an adolescent is trying to test boundaries, which is developmentally normal. But when I hear a child or teen from a hard place say "I won't," my first thought is that they are reacting out of fear. Perhaps they think they will make a fool of themselves in front of peers, or they may not believe adults are trustworthy. So if we respond to a teen's "I won't" with rules and punishment, we will miss a chance to teach them that there are safe adults who want to meet their needs. Whether the child is two, twelve, or eighteen, their behavior is about much more than the behavior we see. If we become tangled up in the behavior, which is the *symptom* of a child's need, we're not going to build trust, connection, or relationship.

One of the greatest concerns for parents and caregivers of teenagers is whether their children are going to be ready for real life. If an adolescent is advancing into his late teens, his caregiver may feel pressure to prepare him for adulthood and the workforce, resulting in more rules and punishment. I believe that many of our punitive practices have grown out of our fear that we haven't prepared teens for real life. But we know from decades of attachment research that if a child can be successful in relationships, they can be ready for real life—and our teens will learn to be successful in relationships only in the context of caring relationships with their caregivers.

The great challenge for people who are serving vulnerable children and teens is to transition from looking at behavior and creating rules to looking at needs and creating relationships. This paradigm shift must occur in our homes, families, schools, and churches. If our children and teens learn to trust safe adults, be comfortable with who they are, and engage in safe, nurturing relationships, they can be prepared for competency as adults.

Lisa

A couple of years ago, my friend Emily's daughter, April, had surgery. April had joined Emily's family as a young teen, and Emily knew the surgery was an opportunity to build trust and connection by meeting her daughter's needs. For two weeks they talked about the soft foods April wanted and the movies they were going to watch together. April even asked to borrow a pair of Emily's pajamas to wear while recovering.

As the day approached, Emily found herself looking forward to nurturing April in a way she hadn't before. Overall, April was a very healthy kid, so aside from making tea for a sore throat or heating up a rice sack for a stomachache, this was a new experience for Emily. It was a whole new level of caring.

With the other kids in school, Emily considered what it would be like to give her daughter undivided attention, help her with pain control, and simply hang out with her.

The night before the procedure, her daughter said, "You know, Mom, I'm kind of looking forward to this. I've never had someone take care of me when I was sick."

I recall a story told to me by a boy who had spent his entire childhood in an orphanage. Some of the children in the orphanage contracted measles. They were quarantined in a dark room and fed special foods. This boy was among them, but in the end, he never got measles. He confided in me that he hadn't been sick—he was simply longing for special attention.

We all want some aspect of this, don't we? When we don't feel well, we want someone to make us tea, encourage us to rest, and cover us with a blanket. Everyone needs to be nurtured.

Emily was able to fill just a bit of that need in sixteen-year-old April's heart. Who could have known that surgery would be such a gift to them?

Key Takeaways

- In many ways, implementing TBRI strategies with teens is easier than with young children.

- Consider both biological and developmental age when relating to teens.

- Teach respect to teens by modeling it first. Be mindful of their histories, and rather than demanding respect from the start, be patient as it grows.

- Similarly, modeling disclosure can help forge honest communication between caregivers and teens.

- Behavioral problems are symptoms of unmet needs—even for teens!

Try It Today

Think of ways to meet your teens' needs. Just as we do with young children, we strive to meet needs in the following ways:

- Meet physical needs with food, water, and sensory input.

- Meet connection needs by putting the relationship at the focus of every interaction.

- Correct behavior and thinking by disarming fear, allowing the authentic child beneath to emerge.

9

Build Your Toolbox

Lisa

One night when I was just about to tuck our boys in bed, I realized my son needed a bath. This was not part of my plan for the evening, and I knew it was going to drag bedtime out, but I forged forward. I put him in the tub and took our other son to the bedroom to read a book. We had a lovely time reading...until I finished the book and he told me that he didn't want to read about Franklin and that I had chosen the wrong book. I told him to stay on his bed and headed to the bathroom to get his brother out of the tub.

I was still maintaining a somewhat cheerful attitude, but I was fading and wishing Russ would come home and take over. I dried my son, helped him put on lotion, and sent him to get pajamas. Together we headed to the bedroom, where the boys began to yell at each other and hit each other. All my resolve failed. I loudly told them to stop yelling and hitting (I know—very effective!) and to get in their beds.

I took a deep breath and went to tuck them in, but the damage was done. One of my sons wouldn't let me touch him. He was crying, and I couldn't calm him. I prayed for him, asked him if he wanted a song (he did not), and then covered him. My other son was more easily calmed, and we had a little snuggle before I left the room.

As Dr. Purvis mentioned earlier, the range of parenting practices that works for healthy, well-attached kids is wide, but it becomes narrower with children from hard places. Some of my children are from hard places, and they don't tolerate sloppy parenting as well as my kids who didn't experience early trauma. This is hard work, but I've learned to press on and work more diligently than ever to bring healing to my children.

I could easily fill several books with more tips and ideas to help you as you parent your children from hard places. I hope the earlier chapters have given you some new ideas. In addition to those, I want to give you some of my best tools to add to your parenting toolbox. Next time you are trying to figure out what to do in a hard moment or when faced with a challenging situation, you may find something you need here. Better still, I hope Dr. Purvis and I have laid the foundation for you to create your own new tools.

When Sad Looks like Mad

I don't know about you, but I'm not fond of those moments when my children stomp away in a huff or cross their arms when they look at me. They are mad, and my initial response is to be irritated. As a child sinks deeper into "being mad," I can feel myself pull away. I get terse and find I don't want to look in their eyes.

This is the crucial moment when I need to stop the "mad cycle" and see it for what it really is—*my child is sad.*

Sadness has woven its way into our children's lives in ways you and I can hardly imagine. Picture a little boy in an orphanage feeling sad. There is no mommy to say, "Honey, come sit with me. Let me hold you." No—when he was sad, he learned that it felt much better to be mad. Mad felt powerful, while sad felt overwhelming and unending.

One eleven-year-old girl grew up where there were few adults to carefully watch over her and guide her through her feelings, so she protected herself by being mad. How did she cope? She turned away from the adults and became bossy toward other children. She felt some relief from the sorrow that had been building up in her heart. She was in control; nobody could hurt her.

Another adopted child, a young teen boy, kept account of wrong-doings, slights, and disappointments, carefully filing them away in his mind. He could hold a grudge like nobody's business. His new adoptive parents were warned that he would refuse to speak to a certain teacher or nanny for days. He commonly refused to eat, work, or make eye contact.

When he joined his adoptive family, they saw he was easily angered, tried to control the other children, and was stubborn beyond reason. As for respect? His parents weren't sure he even knew he was supposed to respect them, because he sure didn't act like it.

> When we remember where kids have come from, we can see past their "mad" behaviors to their "sad" hearts.

When we remember where kids have come from, we can see past their "mad" behaviors to their "sad" hearts. We can hold ourselves in a nurturing mode and keep building those bonds of attachment. We can speak the truth: "Honey, you look angry, but I can see that your heart is actually feeling sad." This is often all it takes to break through the mad facade.

One day we had a moment just like this. I talked frankly with our daughter about my love for her, her dad's love for her, and our desire to fill her heart. I encouraged her to let go of her "mad" behaviors even if that meant feeling her deep, sad feelings. She turned her eyes from me, and I waited. It wasn't long before she said, "Mommy, I'm sorry. I know you love me. I'm just sad my mom died. Your mom didn't die, so you don't know how bad it feels."

She was right. Saying this helped her turn her "mad" into "sad," giving me an opportunity to connect on a deeper level.

Offer a Redo

One night I had an errand to run. I drove a few minutes to a house in town and knocked on the door. A little girl answered with a scowl on her face. "Why are you here?" she demanded.

You can imagine that was not the greeting I was expecting—especially since I was at my friend Michele's and the child was my daughter.

I said, "That is not a respectful or kind way to greet me. Let's shut the door and you can try that again."

I pulled the door shut, stepped back on the porch, paused, and then knocked again.

This time I was greeted with a cool "Hello," but it was a big improvement. I'm not opposed to setting the bar low when I know that striving for more may turn a small situation into a big scene.

I put a big smile on my face and playfully said, "Hi! How was your day? Did you have a good dinner?"

Later, as I talked with Michele, I relayed the incident to her. As we were grabbing our things to go, she cheerfully said, "Hey, let's practice giving your mom a *really* good greeting." My daughter looked up in surprise—even Aunt Michele knew, and now she wanted a redo too! But Michele playfully encouraged her, and I stepped outside the door again. This time when I knocked, my daughter met me with a big, silly smile and an exaggerated greeting. We all laughed.

It's important not to come down with a sledgehammer on small incidents, but it is just as important that we don't ignore them either. Let's set the standard we expect, especially when it comes to respect. The bar may need to be low, but we can slowly move it up and keep believing our children are capable of more. This is what Dr. Purvis has to say about redos:

> By actively replacing misbehavior with correct behavior in your child's memory banks, you can help the child encode competency. A redo "erases" the muscle memory of the failed behavior and gives the child the physical and

emotional experience of substituting a successful one in its place.

And this quote is extremely appropriate:

> A redo can be as simple or complex as needed. As many doors as it took your child to go off course, that's how many you have to revisit and correct each false step.[1]

Say Yes—Teaching Ourselves, Teaching Our Children

A wise parent once told me, "Say yes whenever you can." That wasn't terribly hard when life felt balanced and under control, but all of that changed with the addition of multiple children to our family. Life felt chaotic and unfamiliar. We were deeply tired and barely keeping our heads above water.

I've learned that when life feels out of control, we try to grasp for more control. Sometimes we become less flexible and begin to say no more than we say yes. I remember feeling as if even the smallest thing might send us over the edge, and I didn't want to risk it.

I learned from Dr. Purvis that saying yes is tremendously healing for our children and is a deep point of connection.

As Dr. Purvis explained in an earlier chapter, in the first months of life, babies form memories and are "primed" for future experiences. They cry; we comfort them. They cry; we feed them. They cry; we pick them up and change their diapers. They cry; we come to them. In this way, a baby learns that they have a voice and their needs will be met.

Children with early adversity often experience abuse and neglect. One of our daughters suffered consistent deprivation as a young child. How do I help her make sense of her overwhelming reactions to hunger, fear of trusting and attaching to parents, and a deep sense of competition with siblings? Help from professionals who guide her as she processes her trauma is important.

I can also meet her needs over and over again. When she cries, I need to comfort her. When she is hungry, I need to feed her. When she doesn't trust, I must be trustworthy and safe.

But there is something else I can do every day—I can say yes as often as possible. When she uses her voice to ask for something, big or small, I can meet a need in her heart by saying yes. Dr. Purvis encourages parents to say yes many times each day. This may be inconvenient, and it isn't always possible, but it is one way we can build trust and connection over time.

When a Child Struggles to Say Yes

The power of saying yes works both ways. But I have children who answer nearly everything negatively at first. I try to remind myself that for whatever reason, their brains are wired to answer no first, but if I give them a moment, they'll often answer yes. When I offer something to my son and he says no, if I'm really attuned, I will wait silently for a moment, and he'll often reverse his answer and say yes.

Other times I'll ask him, "Are you sure about that?" and pause for a moment. He catches himself very quickly now, but it took me a long time to figure out his negative answer was somehow instinctive and not his true answer. We must extend lots of grace as our children learn new ways of thinking.

You can play a fun game with your child to help him practice saying yes over and over. Sit close to him, place an empty dish in front of him, and ask, "Would you like an M&M?" (or whatever small treat he likes). Wait silently until he says yes. Then praise him like crazy. "Great job saying yes to Mommy!" and put an M&M in his empty dish. If he'll let you put it in his mouth, that is a huge bonus because feeding each other is a powerful attachment tool. But go with whatever works.

Offer him M&Ms one at a time, as long as he is enjoying it, but be sure to stop before he gets bored or tired. You want this to be fun for your child so he wants to do it again. When we keep the tone light and happy, our kids can relax and learn. He literally needs to create new pathways in his brain so he can trust you enough to say yes.

Dr. Purvis

By now you understand that early trauma changes a child's brain chemistry, and it won't just automatically heal. They need insightful, precise, skillful parenting to bring them to success. Caregivers often ask me, "Where do I start? There's just so much to do, and I don't know where to start!" I know that parenting this way can seem like an incredibly daunting task! Go ahead and stop right here and take a deep breath. The task at hand can seem overwhelming, but there are many simple ways you can start using TBRI today. Your child will never be younger than they are now, so what better time to begin parenting this way?

> Your child will never be younger than they are now, so what better time to begin parenting this way?

All the tools I'll share in this chapter are intended to develop a foundation of trust, which we discussed at length in chapter 3. Our primary goal is to build trust with our children, which happens only when we establish felt safety.

Be a Detective

One of the first things I often ask parents to do is to be detectives. Start to pay careful attention to your child and their behaviors. Be curious about how your child responds to their environment. Do they seek or avoid certain textures? What foods do they avoid? What activities do they avoid? What situations do they overreact to? The answers to all these questions will provide insight into what may be driving fear-based behaviors. Parents will often say, "My child over-reacts." We want those parents to pull out their detective lenses and look at what the child is fearful of in that situation. Oftentimes it is something parents know their child is safe from. So how can the parents help their child *feel* safe?

Because of their histories, vulnerable children can often behave in confusing and seemingly random, unpredictable ways. We often ask parents to keep a journal for a week, recording every behavioral episode of fight, flight, or freeze they dealt with. This practice can be extremely helpful in identifying a pattern to mystifying behaviors. Parents who keep a journal may discover that their child is chronically reactive to hunger, transitions, sounds, or a multitude of other things that could be driving fear. When we become detectives regarding our child's behavior, we learn to empower them, prevent major meltdowns, and build trust.

Transitions

Transitions are some of the most challenging situations for families because they can trigger meltdowns—even in typically developing children. Everyday transitions and major life transitions can be even more difficult for children from hard places. Many times, our children's lives have been chaotic and so full of the unknown that they are desperately trying to stay in control just to survive. Again, we may know their environment is safe and that an upcoming transition is harmless, but a child from a hard place may fall apart at the tiniest change.

Being mindful of the many transitions that occur in a day, parents can be proactive and help their children prepare for these changes. For example, if I'm going to make a transition, I will say, "Hey, buddy, in five minutes we're going to clean up our toys and run an errand." I might come back two minutes later and say, "In three minutes it will be time to clean up and leave the house." We need to help the child prepare for a shift so that they can come along with us. Otherwise, the abrupt change will likely cause a meltdown.

In addition to daily transitions, many life transitions can be scary for our children too, such as starting at a new school, welcoming a new sibling into the home, or moving from one house to another. These major transitions require even more proactive support to help our children feel safe. If such a change is approaching in your family, have conversations during calm times about what's coming. You may even try role-playing so that children can build a motor memory of how to respond during the real event. Be creative about finding ways to gradually introduce a particular transition so your child feels safe and secure.

Be Approachable

Another good way to start is simply by being approachable. Some children find that when they come to the parent, the parent's tone or body language sets them back, and they're not able to go further in their conversation. If you're parenting a child from a hard place, you undoubtedly have many people and things demanding your time and attention. Yet it's important to remember that your child might interpret your busyness as disinterest.

You may feel as if I'm asking you to do the impossible, but there are simple ways that parents can become more approachable even when juggling jobs, multiple children, and various responsibilities. If you're preparing dinner and your child repeatedly asks you to watch what they're doing, try meeting their request with a smile and saying, "Okay, buddy, I can watch you for about one minute, and then I need to finish getting our dinner ready. After dinner I would love to watch some more." A warm smile, eye contact, and just sixty seconds of undivided attention can be so powerful for our children.

These simple acts send the strong message to a child that they are seen, known, and loved. Seemingly small interactions that provide warmth and full attention are actually huge deposits in a trust bank that we're building for a lifetime with this child.

Matching

"Matching" is another important tool you can use to build a bridge to your child. Matching simply means that you position yourself—your body, your voice, your attention—in a way that matches your child. For example, if your child is sitting with their legs crossed and playing, you can sit the same way as you play with them. Behavioral matching sends a strong message of connection to a child.

This comes with a caveat: At first it may feel scary to the child for you to come into their space, so be aware they might change their body position very quickly. That's okay—and even normal. Try not to be distressed if your child thwarts your attempts to connect with them in this way. That just means you need to go a little slower as you continue to build trust. Try to match in ways that are not as conspicuous. If the child is using a soft voice, you can too. Or if your child is using a playful voice, you can do the same. Even matching their voice is a very powerful bridge to children.

In one of our camps several years ago, one child who has a history of extreme trauma would not play with anybody. My colleague Dr. David Cross sat down and said to this precious child, "Can I play with you?" The child said no. So Dr. Cross sat down beside him and started playing alone with a toy car. When the little guy moved his car in a certain way, Dr. Cross would do something similar. When the little guy made some sound effects, Dr. Cross made those noises too. After just a couple of minutes, this little one turned to Dr. Cross and asked, "You wanna play?" This is a wonderful example of entering a child's space carefully. Try starting with just your voice or some subtle body language.

Matching is not only powerful for the child, but its benefits also extend to the parent. I find myself becoming more present with the child when I'm aware and try to match their voice or body language. Now I'm listening to my child's tone. Now I'm looking at my child's posture. It does as much for me as it does for my child. This simple tool can cause you to feel deeply connected.

Share Power and Give Choices

In the best situations, children experience some structure and predictability, giving them an appropriate sense of control over their environment. If a child's world is predictable, they tend to fare better. But for the at-risk child, predictability and appropriate levels of control must be established as we build felt safety. Some parents may feel anxious when I ask them to think of ways they can share power with their children. Take a deep breath and remember that by sharing power, you prove it is yours to share.

As we mentioned earlier, a terrific way for parents to share appropriate levels of power is to give choices. Sometimes we give choices when we are correcting behavior, but for now I want to focus on giving choices to share power and build trust. By letting a child decide whether they'd like to play or have a snack first, or would prefer to use crayons or markers, I communicate that their voice matters and that a safe adult cares about their wants and needs. The wonderful thing about offering choices is that you can do it in almost any situation—even scenarios where there seem to be no choices. For example, if your child has a doctor's appointment that cannot be missed, offer the choice of an activity before or after the appointment.

As you give simple choices throughout the day, you make your child's world predictable. Giving choices is an unassuming way to partner with your child, give them a voice, and build trust. If our child came from an environment that was chaotic and out of control, choices help them feel safe and in control. Children also learn to trust the loving adult who is caring for them. By giving choices, we partner with our children in the relationship and empower them to have an appropriate level of control by deciding what happens next. Together you are making their world predictable, and in doing so, vast gains can be made in their behavior.

Compromises

Similar to choices, compromises can be very powerful tools not only for helping a child behave better but also for helping a child know that you hear their voice.

Please understand—I'm not talking about a seven-year-old negotiator who can talk you out of everything you have! Obviously, sometimes you can make a compromise and sometimes you cannot. I'm simply pointing out that a compromise helps our children trust and develop social skills.

I always recommend a few general guiding principles for compromises. I use compromises with children to "keep the train moving"—to avoid a standoff, power struggle, or behavioral freeze—or if I think a child can do part (but not all) of what I want them to do. My goal is always to keep the train moving toward connection.

I typically use a compromise when I've offered choices but the child is not able to choose. After giving the child enough time to process the options, I might nudge them in the right direction by asking, "Are you asking for a compromise?" The child will often need help coming up with a compromise. Remember, we want to give them *appropriate* levels of control. Here's a simple example of how a compromise might play out.

Parent: It's time to stop playing and take a bath.

Child: I don't want to!

Parent: I hear you, buddy. It's hard to stop playing when we're having fun. Do you want to pick up your toys on your own, or would you like for me to help you?

Child: Neither! I want to keep playing!

Parent: It sounds like you're asking for a compromise. Could you use your good words and ask me with respect?

Child: Could I play some more before my bath?

Parent: Okay, how about this? Let's set a timer for five more minutes, and you can play until the timer goes off. My end of the bargain is that I let you play for five more minutes, and your end of the bargain is that when the timer goes off, it's time for the bath. Do we have a deal?

This is a very "clean" example of how a compromise could unfold. I encourage you to practice compromises through role play in calm times to build the skill.

Redos

I want to remind you again about the power of redos. I recommend a behavioral redo as an effective way to teach new behaviors. A redo simply gives the child the opportunity to try something again. To a child who grabs a crayon out of my hand, I might say, "Please give it to me and use your words to ask for it." I can coach the child to ask, "Could I please have that crayon?" and respond by saying, "Wow, that was great using your words. Of course you can have that crayon." A redo is a chance for the child to do the behavior again, do it right, feel good about doing it right, and be praised for doing it right. This builds their confidence and teaches them essential skills.

By utilizing a redo instead of giving a lecture about your child's behavior, you give your child a motor memory of doing something the right way. As developmental scientists, my colleagues and I know that a motor memory can trump a cognitive memory, so the more a child practices doing the right things with their bodies, the more successful they're going to be doing those same things again and again.

Use Your Toolbox to Build Your Child's Toolbox

We've spent this chapter talking about ways we can build your parenting toolbox. Remember that these tools are designed for you to build connection, help your child feel safe, and provide them with tools to cope. If you have to take a behavioral strategy away from a child, always be sure to give them a skill in its place. Remember that your child's behaviors are survival strategies. Asking them to lay aside the only tools they've had without handing them replacement tools will only drive fear-based behaviors.

I'll use the example of showing respect. We don't say "You cannot talk to me like that" without first teaching our daughter or son how to use words respectfully. We might say, "I will always listen to you, but please use respect." When you take away the tools your child used to get her needs met before she joined your family, you must replace them with more effective strategies.

Celebrate the Need

One of the most important things I ever tell parents is to celebrate their children's needs. Learn to delight in your child's need for you and their expression of that need. If they come to you in the night and say, "I'm afraid," you can celebrate that they're telling you they're afraid. Praise your child for telling you about their fear and create a plan to help them feel safe. Perhaps you could put a sleeping bag or some blankets by your bed and say, "Anytime you're afraid and you want to come to my room, come wake me up, curl in bed with me, and cuddle a little while. Then you can sleep right beside me in your special sleeping bag, and I'll hold your hand."

Whatever it is that our child is fearful of, let's celebrate their need. Let's celebrate their trust. And let's continue to earn that trust by creating an environment of felt safety.

Lisa

Each summer, our family takes a vacation on Whidbey Island in

Washington state. We spend our days exploring tide pools, sailing a small catamaran, and playing. Of course, I spend many of my hours fixing meals, doing laundry, and managing the crew, but it is a wonderful time for our family to enjoy one another.

One evening we gathered around the campfire under a starry sky, roasting marshmallows and talking. The older boys had come for the weekend and brought a guitar, which they passed among themselves, leading us in silly songs. Our youngest son fell asleep in my arms, and another snuggled on Russ's lap. It was a rare, peaceful moment for our busy and sometimes chaotic family.

As it grew later, we took the younger children in and began tucking them into bed. Our daughter came to me in the kitchen, wrapped her arms around my waist, leaned her head against me, and said, "That was the best time of my entire life. I love being in our family now." You can imagine how much that filled my heart. These were hard-earned words for both of us.

Keeping her close, offering redos, saying yes as much as we can, and looking beyond her actions to her heart have brought more healing than we ever imagined. She is woven into our family.

Key Takeaways

- Be a detective about your child's behavior.
- Be mindful of transitions and practice them proactively.
- Be approachable.
- Practice behavioral matching to forge connection.
- Share power and give choices.
- Consider compromises.
- Offer redos to create motor memory.
- Celebrate your child's needs.

Try It Today

Your child will never be younger than they are right now. Choose one thing to practice and start today!

Part 3

Hope and Strength for the Journey

10

Take Care of Yourself

Lisa

It was summer. We should have been enjoying the sunshine, going swimming, and family time, but the truth was we were having one hard day after another. We were depleted. Within minutes of arriving home from a family gathering, everything fell apart. Despite my best efforts, the break in our routine had been dysregulating for our daughter, and she was struggling.

Hours later, when the crisis was over and the children were finally asleep, Russ and I lay next to each other, holding hands in the dark. All I could say was, "We're okay. We're okay," as tears ran down my face.

The years of loving and caring for our daughter were taking a toll on us.

The next morning, we signed her up for day camp. She needed more structure to her days than I could provide, and her siblings were desperate for more of my attention. Additionally, I needed to think clearly and make a better plan for meeting her needs. I was simply getting through the days.

While we were walking this hard road, I was still responsible for the normal things of life, especially caring for my family. Our refrigerator was nearly empty, but making a grocery list when my mind was full and my heart was heavy was no small task. I found myself rewashing loads of laundry I'd forgotten in the washer because I couldn't remember to transfer them to the dryer.

Russ and I weren't sleeping well. I'd wake up in the night to find him already awake, unable to let go of the stress and fears.

During one of our counseling appointments, our therapist said, "Lisa, it's like you're being pecked to death by ducks all day." My children's needs were great, and I was completely exhausted. Parenting kids with developmental trauma and special needs is a long and often challenging journey. It requires us to work hard, be creative and diligent, and truly persevere as we meet our children's needs.

The knowledge Dr. Purvis and I have shared and the tools we've given provide a foundation for parenting children from hard places. Trust and connection give our children the greatest hope for healing. But this is not a vending-machine formula. Using the perfect tool does not always produce the perfect result.

Our children are human, with good days and bad. They are unique and have layers of complexity because of early adverse experiences. With trust and connection as our foundation, Russ and I have explored many therapies and tools for helping our children heal, often traveling long distances and making significant sacrifices for the whole family.

Amid this parenting marathon, we also need practical tools and tips to keep ourselves going. Deep weariness can lead to exhaustion and discouragement, which hinder our ability to nurture our children. When we're tired, it's difficult to maintain empathy and parent with connection in mind. We often default to the way we were raised or how we parented our other children, which are not what our kids from hard places need.

Caring for Ourselves

The good news is that simple tools are available for caring for our minds and bodies and for renewing our hope and strength. When we care for ourselves, we create healthy brain chemistry, giving us the capacity for healthier relationships.

Physical Health

We need to care for our minds by taking care of our bodies. We must not neglect basic health screenings or ignore symptoms requiring medical attention. Saying for months, "I'll go to the doctor if it gets *really* bad" may result in a much bigger problem.

I spoke with an adoptive mom whose tooth had been hurting. She was so busy caring for her children that she began altering how she ate and taking increasing amounts of over-the-counter pain medication. But eventually the pain became unbearable. She realized how many months had passed with this problem and scheduled an appointment with her dentist, who recommended a root canal.

The funny thing is that when she told me this story, I replied that the same thing had happened to me in the months following the arrival of our children from Ethiopia. I had no time to think about caring for myself, and I, too, paid a big price for neglecting my health.

Regular exercise is extremely helpful. Run a marathon if you like, but taking walks will also give you the necessary boost in brain chemistry and support good health. The rhythmic nature of walking is calming, and being outdoors is a huge bonus. There's something about moving, observing the world, and breathing that restores us.

If you have little ones, put them in a stroller and take them along. It will be good for them too.

The best way to add a walk to my days is to tie it to another time when I need to leave the house. For instance, dropping the boys off at school and immediately taking a walk before going home works well for me. Walking while they're at a sports practice is also good.

Sleep

Getting adequate sleep was a problem for many years simply

because our most hypervigilant children didn't sleep. When kids don't sleep, parents don't sleep. For a long time, we rolled out sleeping bags on our bedroom floor for children to quietly crawl into if they woke in the night. Of course, many nights they woke us, but overall, we got more sleep by letting them stay near us.

> Lack of sleep leads to lack of self-discipline, patience, and hope.

It's also tempting to stay up late after the kids are in bed. We feel like we haven't gotten a break all day, and it's finally quiet. The problem is, it's easy to get so tired that we stay up even later because it seems like too much work to go to bed. We mindlessly watch Netflix or scroll through social media on our phones.

Lack of sleep leads to lack of self-discipline, patience, and hope. One of the most helpful things I do is getting ready for bed when I'm getting the kids ready; even if I stay up for another hour or two, I can easily go to bed when I'm tired.

Establishing a simple evening routine also helps our minds and bodies settle at the end of the day. Starting the dishwasher, setting up the next morning's coffee, getting ready for bed, checking the next day's schedule, and putting my phone away are all messages that the day is ending and it's time to sleep.

Completing a Task

Setting aside time to focus on one task and complete it is good for our minds. I feel mentally stronger and more at peace when I accomplish a task. Our lives are so scattered with needs, and we're moving from one thing to the next so quickly, that everything feels undone.

I'm a list maker and love checking things off, but in times of intense parenting and stress, the list grows impossibly long. My solution is to choose one to three top goals for a day, even if they're as simple as scheduling an appointment or making a grocery list.

Accomplishing these few goals is a small thing I can manage when life feels overwhelming.

Restful Thinking

Letting your mind rest and be unfocused for a bit of time each day is good for you. With so much to accomplish in the hours we have, we're inclined to be productive until we collapse. Believe it or not, daydreaming is restorative for our overworked brains.

Sometimes I stand on my back porch and look out at the view for a few minutes. I breathe deeply, usually trying to ignore the noises in the kitchen behind the closed door.

Try going for a walk without listening to a book or podcast, and simply take in the sounds around you. If by some miracle you're in the car alone, leave the radio off, and don't make phone calls like I often do (hands-free, of course!). Embrace rare moments of quiet, and resist the urge to fill them.

Focused Attention

In contrast to restful thinking, when our minds are free to wander, focused attention is the practice of concentrating on one thing in the present moment. For example, we can become aware of part of our bodies, a feeling, or a thought.

We can quiet the thoughts running wild in our minds by focusing on one thing. So often we're juggling lots of details with schedules and needs to meet, and we don't slow down and simply breathe. This often leads to anxious thoughts and fears about our children and our futures. Focused attention allows your brain to rest from the racing thoughts.

Play

Fun and play often feel like luxuries when we're raising children with complex needs. True confession: I'm not good at playing, but I've learned that being spontaneous and having fun are good for our brains and bodies. Playing a card game or dancing in the kitchen with your kids boosts your brain chemistry, and your kids will like it too.

While it doesn't come easily, I never regret time spent playing with my kids. When we laugh together, we feel a deeper connection, and my heart feels lighter.

Gratitude

Reflecting on the good amid the hard is very helpful. I keep a small journal where I record something I'm thankful for each day. This has been a powerful practice for me. My mind drifts easily to difficult challenges, things that are going wrong, and hurdles that seem impossible to overcome. When I pause to think about it, however, there is always something I can acknowledge as good, even if it's as simple as hot water, the scent of a tangerine, or my child smiling at me. Reading through my gratitude journal reminds me I'm surrounded by gifts of love and beauty.

Connecting

Of all the helpful tools on this journey, the one that has contributed the most to my emotional health is community. People who understand my life, my kids, and my feelings (even my tears) are the greatest gifts. Connecting with friends in person is wonderful, but it's often hard to even get out the door.

I've met some of my best friends through the world of adoption and foster care. They may be spread out around the country, but we connect regularly by phone or through social media.

Amid our parenting struggles, we can easily feel discouraged and even ashamed. Sometimes I feel like a complete failure and am convinced I will never be able to be the mom my kids need. My friends remind me to be realistic about the challenges and be kind to myself.

We are not perfect parents. We're all just doing the best we can as we parent children with unique and significant needs.

Professional Help

Parenting children with traumatic pasts may bring up unresolved issues from our own childhoods that get in the way of parenting our kids. Processing this with the support of a good therapist can be extremely helpful. Additionally, marriages may come under severe strain when parenting at this level. Seek help from a counselor if you're struggling to stay connected under the weight of your family's needs.

It's important to note that foster and adoptive parents may experience clinical depression and secondary trauma. Seek professional help from a therapist and physician if you think this might be happening to you. Therapy is good for nearly all of us at times, but it's essential for parents whose brains and bodies are exhausted to the point of despair or who have become so triggered from trauma that they're struggling to relate to their children in a healing way.

There is no shame in seeking professional help; in fact, it's wise. Your family needs you to be as healthy as possible, and self-care alone may not be enough.

Dr. Purvis

Throughout this book, I've touched on the principles of Trust-Based Relational Intervention (TBRI) and how empowering your child's body, connecting with their spirit, and correcting their behavior can bring deep healing to your child's wounded heart. Now I'd like you to use those same principles to take care of yourself. Attend to your own journey of healing so you can lead your child on theirs.

As Lisa mentioned, parents and caregivers of children who have experienced adversity often become so consumed by their children's many needs that they unintentionally neglect their own. Furthermore, helping our children heal can often lead to secondary trauma in parents and caregivers. The National Child Traumatic Stress Network defines secondary trauma this way: "Secondary Traumatic

Stress refers to the presence of PTSD symptoms caused by at least one indirect exposure to traumatic material."[1]

For sufferers of secondary traumatic stress, or secondary trauma, compassion fatigue is often an accompanying issue. The National Child Traumatic Stress Network defines compassion fatigue as "the exhaustion and negative emotional, physiological, biological and cognitive effects resulting from the cumulative effects of empathetic engagement with and secondary exposure to, trauma."[2]

Compassion fatigue affects those in helping professions as well as parents of children from hard places. Please don't feel ashamed for experiencing compassion fatigue. Acknowledge your feelings and begin to explore what your body, soul, and spirit need to heal and regain resilience.

Connecting

We apply the TBRI Connecting Principles with the children in our care to help them build trusting relationships and find their voices. You can reframe the Connecting Principles for yourself to find your own trusting relationships and your own voice.

The Connecting Principles have two sets of strategies: mindfulness and engagement. Mindfulness starts with knowing yourself. I often encourage parents, caregivers, and professionals to develop a daily mindfulness practice to help them become more present, aware, and available to the people in their lives. Mindfulness is simply the practice of being aware, and it can take different forms. Many books and online resources are available for cultivating mindfulness, but here are a few of my favorite exercises, which may help you develop this important skill.

- Take a walk barefoot in the grass. Notice how cool and soft the grass is. Give your full attention to the grass and notice how your body feels in it.
- Practice being aware of your breath. Between appointments

or daily tasks, take two or three minutes and rest comfortably. Feel your back resting against the chair. Feel the seat of the chair beneath you. Lean back in the chair and breathe, focusing on your breath. If your mind wanders, simply breathe, and gently bring your focus back to your breath. Focus on your shoulders as you breathe in and out, allowing them to relax.

- Practice being aware of your body. Sit in a chair, and slowly coax your body to relax, beginning with your feet and continuing all the way up to your head. Focus on one body part at a time, tensing that part and then relaxing it, then moving on to the next body part. When you reach your neck and head, spend a few minutes breathing, relaxing into your body.

> Make it a goal to pause and say yes when someone asks if they can help rather than automatically saying no and insisting you have things handled.

The next part of the TBRI Connecting Principles is engagement, which is about connectedness to others. Research tells us that connections are essential to overall well-being. Think about the people in your life who offer the most connection and support. In chapter 2, we talked about the four skills important for meaningful relationships, one of which is receiving care. Although it is often difficult for individuals who are caring for children with many unique needs, it's essential to allow others to take part in our own self-care. Make it a goal to pause and say yes when someone asks if they can help rather than automatically saying no and insisting you have things handled. As Lisa suggested, find people who understand your journey and can walk alongside you.

Empowering

Let's consider ways to empower ourselves by meeting our own physical needs. Many parents and caregivers who serve children from hard places are experiencing secondary trauma and chronic stressors that negatively impact the body. Just as we strive to create a healing environment where children can feel safe and have their physical needs met, try to create an environment where you can have moments of respite from any chronic stressors. Here are a few suggestions for creating a healing environment.

Sleep

Many health professionals will encourage you to focus on sleep first. Sleep and the capacity to sleep deeply have direct impacts on cognition, physical health, immune function, and resilience. Lack of sleep has many physical consequences, including decreased cognition, ADHD-like symptoms, impaired judgment, and decreased immune function. If your child requires lots of attention during the night, try taking turns caring for them with your spouse to increase your sleep.

Telling the parent of a child from a hard place to get plenty of sleep is about as helpful as telling parents of a newborn baby to get a good night's rest—many times it's just not realistic! But when you do get the chance to sleep, make sure your sleeping environment is conducive to rest. Lower the lights in your home an hour or so before bedtime. Limit your time on blue screens, such as smart phones, tablets, computers, or television, to allow your body to naturally release melatonin. Keep your bedroom simply furnished and decorated so your mind can relax when you enter the space. Consider using a sound machine or essential oil diffuser with a calming scent to make the room especially soothing.

Hydration

Hydration has been proven to be highly correlated with cognitive ability and metabolism. If you are even just 15 percent dehydrated, cognitive function declines. While there are many rules of thumb about drinking a certain number of glasses of water per day, I recommend a much simpler (albeit slightly more graphic) tip for checking your hydration level: Your urine should be clear and odorless. If you're urinating frequently and it is clear and odorless, you are hydrated!

Blood Sugar

Blood sugar is a powerful regulator of the body. The human brain weighs 3 percent of your body weight, yet it consumes 60 percent of the glucose in your body. For that reason, eating foods that stabilize rather than spike blood sugar will help with cognitive, behavioral, and emotional stability throughout the day. Insulin receptor sites are often altered in children with histories of harm, and the same is true of individuals who experience chronic stress. Choosing foods that are low on the glycemic index can help regulate blood sugar.

Foods high in protein will help stabilize the blood sugar, particularly at bedtime. We know from research that children and adults who have chronic stress may have closely correlated cortisol and blood sugar levels. So when blood sugar lowers during the night, they may wake up, activating their cortisol and further disrupting sleep. Try having a couple of slices of turkey or a spoonful of peanut butter about an hour before bedtime to prevent blood sugar lows in the night.

Physical Activity

We encourage our children to have a physical activity or sensory exercise every two hours, and I encourage adults to also build opportunities for physical activity into the day. Physical movement helps organize the brain and releases endorphins, which elevate our moods. Even a simple walk is a wonderful activity that helps us use both sides of our brains. Taking a walk with your child can have tremendous benefits for both of you, or perhaps you could walk while taking care of such tasks as returning phone calls and scheduling appointments.

Correcting

Please know that applying the Correcting Principles to yourself does *not* mean focusing on the things that aren't going perfectly in your family. As we explore how the Correcting Principles apply to self-care and combating compassion fatigue, let's think in terms of proactive and responsive strategies for correcting our thinking and the lenses through which we see our children.

Much of what we've talked about regarding the TBRI Empowering and Connecting Principles will make up proactive strategies to help you cope with the daily stressors in your life. Ask yourself, "How can I find more joy and laughter in my life?" and make changes to cultivate more joy and peace in your world.

Responsive strategies for self-care will help us notice the way we respond in the middle of a difficult moment with our children. Spend time reflecting on interactions that didn't go the way you'd hoped. Ask a counselor or trusted friend who understands your child to help you think through what went wrong and how you could respond differently in the future.

If you find yourself viewing your child as manipulative or behaving out of willful disobedience, stop and breathe. Spend a few minutes reflecting on your child's history and its connection to their behavior. Gently remind yourself to reframe your child's behavior as an unmet need rather than attack against you.

One final thought on the responsive strategies: Pay attention to the way you respond to your mistakes. Instead of beating yourself up for interactions that go less than perfectly, try to speak to yourself the way you would to a dear friend in the same situation. Learning to parent this way is no small task. Celebrate your successes and give yourself permission to go slowly. Small lifestyle changes are key when it comes to self-care. Be gentle with yourself and choose one thing to focus on at a time.

Lisa

Let me illustrate the importance of community more clearly. One night my young daughter was very distressed. What had started as irritability had advanced to yelling, slamming doors, and then all-out rage.

I was trying everything I knew to calm my daughter while also keeping her separated from her siblings, who were distressed by her behavior. When I tried to approach her in a gentle, loving manner, she became more agitated. I tried words, food, water...but nothing reached her.

I was exhausted and scared, struggling to stay calm so I could help her regulate. Amid the chaos, I called one of my best friends. The moment Kathleen answered, she could hear things were not going well. I cried as I explained what was happening, and she spoke words of wisdom and kindness to me.

Then, through her wailing and tears, my daughter choked out the words "Tell Miss Kathleen to pray for me."

My daughter agreed to crawl into bed, and I held the phone to her ear. My dear friend prayed for her, and as she did, my daughter began to quiet, her wailing turning to deep, shaky breaths. Unsure if she would allow me to come close, I slowly sat down on the side of the bed. Completely exhausted, she began to drift toward sleep, and I gently rubbed her back.

Years later, when I think of that night, tears still fill my eyes. I'm profoundly grateful for friends who love us, who never judge my kids, and who always remind me that we can persevere in the name of love for the sake of our children.

Key Takeaways

- Connect with yourself and others by...

    practicing mindful awareness

    engaging in supportive community

- Empower your body by...

    meeting your needs for sleep, hydration, and
    balanced blood sugar

    prioritizing physical activity

- Correct your thinking and give yourself grace by...

    reflecting on what's difficult

    making a plan for implementing one small change
    at a time

Try It Today

Identify one area of self-care to practice today. Choose from the list below or think of your own:

    care for your physical health

    get adequate sleep

    complete a task

    let your mind rest

    practice focused attention

    play as a family

    practice gratitude

Conclusion

Lisa

It's been fourteen years since Russ and I entered the world of parenting children from hard places. What a journey it's been—incredibly hard and incredibly rewarding. Our lives have changed in so many ways, we hardly resemble the family we were before.

There was a time when I grieved this lost family, but I see the beauty in the family we've become. All of my children amaze me. They've learned to love in hard circumstances and to have empathy for people who are struggling. Their worlds are so much bigger because of adoption and foster care.

> There was a time when I grieved this lost family, but I see the beauty in the family we've become.

This is what I know:

- Healing is not all-or-nothing for our kids with early trauma. There are many small steps along the way.

- Our job is to press on even when it doesn't appear that anything will turn out the way we'd like.

- We must not look at parenting with a mindset of success or failure.

- Parenting requires true patience—patience for the long haul. Think years, not months.

- We need to give our kids and ourselves grace on this long attachment journey. We can have satisfying relationships and love deeply even if the secure attachment we yearn for hasn't come yet.

- As they become young adults, our children must travel their own journeys of healing. Our role is to support them while also giving them space to do this.

- Our worth and value aren't tied to our kids' progress. Likewise, their worth and value aren't tied to making us look successful as parents!

- Shame will steal our joy and the ability to appreciate our kids for who they are if we let it. Let's be kind to our children and ourselves because, well, sometimes life is just hard.

Dr. Purvis

We hope you've finished this book feeling encouraged and inspired to be a change agent of deep healing in your child's life. But it's also possible that you're feeling overwhelmed or discouraged. If you're feeling discouraged, I have good news for you: There are no terminal mistakes in parenting. As a matter of fact, we know from research that making mistakes is actually quite healthy. If we make a mistake—perhaps we're too harsh or aren't responsive to our child's need—but we are attuned to our child and repair that mistake, there is a release of dopamine, and a new synaptic connection forms in the brain. Giving yourself a redo can create new pathways in the brain!

> Trust-based parenting takes consistency, persistence, and connection, and the payoffs are immense.

Please know that we can always build trust with a child when we realize our mistakes and change how we parent. Just as we've asked you to give your child room to grow and learn, we ask that you apply the same principle to yourself.

Trust-based parenting takes consistency, persistence, and connection, and the payoffs are immense. As you move forward in your parenting journey, remember these things:

- Errors are not terminal, but failure to repair a mistake could damage your relationship with your child. So be intentional about repair.

- Find little ways to celebrate small victories along the way.

- Surround yourself with people who understand your journey and who are compassionate about your pain.

I've worked with children all over the world with varying degrees of trauma in their histories, and I've never yet seen a child who couldn't experience dramatic levels of healing. The greatest predictor of a child's capacity for healing is a safe, nurturing adult who can help them learn to trust. It is my deepest desire that these insights will bring healing, joy, and hope to your family.

Lisa

Parenting children with early trauma requires us to learn new ways of living and loving. The learning curve is steep and takes tremendous effort. Press on, my friend! You are doing good work, parenting in complex circumstances. Your children are worth every bit of the energy you put into learning new ways of parenting them and guiding them toward wholeness.

As you bring healing to hearts and minds, you're changing the lives of your children and future generations. You're doing something incredible. You really are.

Building trust and attachment with your children may be far more challenging than you imagined, but run the race with courage. We're cheering you on!

A Tribute to Dr. Karyn Purvis

by Olive Talley

May 31, 1949—April 12, 2016

Dr. Karyn Purvis was the Rees-Jones Director and cofounder of the Karyn Purvis Institute of Child Development at Texas Christian University in Fort Worth, Texas. She was also the cocreator of Trust-Based Relational Intervention®, the coauthor of the bestselling book in the adoption genre, *The Connected Child*, and a passionate and effective advocate for children. She coined the term "children from hard places" to describe the children she loved and served—those who have suffered trauma, abuse, neglect, or other adverse conditions early in life. Her research-based philosophy for healing children who have been harmed centered on earning trust and building deep emotional connections to anchor and empower them.

Among academics, Dr. Purvis was a respected researcher who demonstrated how the right environment can improve a child's behavior, neurochemistry, and life trajectory. Among parents, she was an authoritative speaker and writer and trainer. Many adoptive parents, who marveled at her innate ability to playfully connect with and see the real heart of a child, revered her as a "child whisperer." To the thousands of children whose lives she touched, she was warmly known as "Miss Karyn, the queen of bubble gum!"

A mother, grandmother, foster parent, pastor's wife, and developmental psychologist, Dr. Purvis devoted her life to serving children. In the past decade, she and her team at the Karyn Purvis Institute of Child Development inspired tens of thousands of parents, professionals, foreign dignitaries, political leaders, orphanage and adoption workers, lawmakers, judges, and child advocates around the world, teaching them about the need for trauma-informed care and trust-based interventions for vulnerable children.

"If I could tell you my dream for every child in the world, it would be to imagine a world where the cry of every child is met by a loving compassionate adult," she once told an interviewer. "Giving voice to children is the heart and soul of what we do."

At age 47, as her sons began college, Karyn returned to school to complete her undergraduate degree. In 1999, she and her mentor and advisor, Dr. David R. Cross, offered a summer camp for adopted children as a research project toward her doctorate in child development. Parents reported dramatic improvements with their children and clamored for more help. That camp became the Hope Connection, and after more research and more camps, Karyn earned her PhD in psychology at the age of 53.

Just a few years later, in 2005, TCU formally created the Karyn Purvis Institute of Child Development to house and to advance the work of Dr. Purvis and Dr. Cross. Over the course of the next decade, they teamed up to write their acclaimed book, *The Connected Child*, and to create a holistic, comprehensive, research-based approach to healing vulnerable children called Trust-Based Relational Intervention (TBRI).

In just over a decade under Dr. Purvis's leadership, the institute has reached an audience spanning the United States and more than 25 other countries around the world. Her passion and novel, research-proven insight led to interviews and news coverage in *Newsweek*, the *Chicago Tribune*, *The Dallas Morning News*, the *Fort Worth Star-Telegram*, KERA Radio, *Dateline NBC*, Focus on the Family, *Parents Magazine*, *Fort Worth Weekly*, and countless other media outlets, blogs, and webinars.

In 2008, then-governor Rick Perry appointed Dr. Purvis to chair a statewide committee tasked with raising standards for children in foster care. The National Council on Adoption honored Dr. Purvis with the title of Distinguished Fellow in Adoption and Child Development. She received the James Hammerstein Award, the T. Berry Brazelton award for Infant Mental Health Advocacy, the Health Care Hero award from the *Dallas Business Journal*, and numerous other awards and honors for her work on behalf of children.

What mattered most to Dr. Purvis, however, was not the accolades, but seeing real change and healing in the lives of children and their families. She was driven to make a difference, and this work became her life purpose. She believed passionately and fervently in the power of hope, knowledge, and prayer.

"I had strength from my faith, and I had the confidence that serving children was my calling," she told an interviewer.

"If I have planted and farmed the soil well, those who come after me, and after them and after them, will be wiser, better equipped, and more able to continue our mission, which is not rhetoric for our institute," Dr. Purvis said. "We truly are learning to change the world for children."

In late 2016, the Institute changed its name to Karyn Purvis Institute of Child Development to honor her life and legacy. The work of Dr. Purvis continues to flourish at the institute, where her team remains fiercely committed to changing the world for children.

Acknowledgments

My deepest gratitude goes to the late Dr. Karyn Purvis. In 2012, I was quite nervous as I presented my idea for this book over our hotel breakfast. To my delight, she embraced the concept of a book blending current research with my parenting experiences.

We spent months emailing chapters back and forth between Texas and Idaho. Dr. Purvis's assistant, Emmelie Pickett, kept us organized as we worked.

Dr. Purvis was in treatment for cancer when we began the project. While she took a sabbatical to focus on her health, I continued making progress on the chapters. When she was well again, we continued working as a team. In the fall of 2014, Dr. Purvis had a recurrence of cancer, yet even in her email sharing this news, she discussed chapters we were working on.

In December 2014, Russ and I were in a car accident with our daughter Kalkidan. Tragically, she did not survive. Writing those words still pierces my heart and feels unreal. Once again Dr. Purvis and I took a break from the book, but I was determined to finish it in honor of Kalkidan, who changed our lives forever when she joined our family at the age of five.

When I had recovered enough to write, we pressed on. Dr. Purvis continued to write, even calling during a chemotherapy treatment to discuss chapters with me. To the great sorrow of everyone who loved her, Dr. Purvis passed away on April 12, 2016.

I could not have completed this book without Emmelie Pickett, who stepped in to bring order to Karyn's drafts and tie up many loose ends. Thank you from the bottom of my heart, Emmelie.

Also essential was the support of the Purvis family, who believed this book should be completed because it was their mother's desire to put it into your hands and hearts. Dwayne, Lou, and Jeremy, what an honor it is to be entrusted with your mother's final written work. Thank you.

Many thanks to the staff at the Karyn Purvis Institute of Child Development, where Dr. Purvis's work continues to thrive. Thanks to Dr. David Cross for his support of the project, to Dr. Casey Call for reading the manuscript and providing feedback, and to Dr. Sheri Parris for verifying the research mentioned in this book.

Dear friends read portions of the manuscript and answered numerous texts about details. For this, special thanks go to Kathleen Hamer, Emily Wynsma, and Melissa Corkum.

Jayne Schooler, Beth Guckenberger, and Sherrie Eldridge helped me through the "how to write a good book proposal and find a publisher" phase. Thank you for all you give to the adoption community and vulnerable children. Thank you also to Terri Coley, who believed in this book and supported its completion after Dr. Purvis passed away.

Thank you to Harvest House Publishers and Kyle Hatfield, who took a chance on this book. I hope to make you proud! Mike and Kristin Berry, your introduction to Kyle was instrumental. As fellow authors, you know how much it means to me. Thank you also to Gene Skinner, the most encouraging editor a first-time author could have.

To my One Thankful Mom readers, I can't thank you enough for journeying with me as I've worked to make sense of my life and adoption/fostering journey through writing. You've taught me so much and are truly the most beautiful readers.

To Michele Dickison, Signe Schumaker, Beth Littlejohn, and Jenny Story: You came alongside me in the hardest season of my life, and I'm eternally grateful. Abbey Bisschop, thank you for answering your phone when I called. Mark and Emily Barr, we're so glad God used you to start us on this path.

Thank you to Deborah Gray, who offered us compassion alongside tools to parent our children. It was worth every mile we traveled to work with you. Heartfelt gratitude to the team at Intermountain, especially Kristen Berg, Ashley Browne, Schuyler Freeman, Kelby Garman, and Chris Haughee.

Dan and Kathleen Hamer, I hardly have words to express what a gift you are to us. Michael and Marybeth Johnston, thank you for loving our kids and sharing our journey.

To my parents, Richard and Mary, and my sisters, Laura and Elizabeth: I love you. Thank you for believing I really would publish a book.

To my children by birth, adoption, and foster care: You are living this journey with me. You continue to teach me about attachment, trust, nurture, trauma, healing, resilience, and how to be a mother. You are the most amazing people, and I love you with all my heart.

To Russ: You described it well when you said our family was on a familiar, safe path when we took a leap of faith and changed our direction by adopting and fostering children. What a journey this is. We may not have a peaceful, empty nest like many of our friends, but we are rich in love.

Most of all, unending gratitude to Jesus, who loves us and has carried us through it all.

Notes

Chapter 1: Understand the Foundation of Attachment

1. Alan L. Sroufe, "Attachment and Development: A Prospective, Longitudinal Study from Birth to Adulthood," *Attachment and Human Development* 7, no. 4 (2005): 349–67.

2. Sroufe, "Attachment," 349–67.

3. Arthur Becker-Weidman, "Effects of Early Maltreatment on Development: A Descriptive Study Using the Vineland Adaptive Behavior Scales-II," *Child Welfare* 88, no. 2 (2009): 137–61.

Chapter 2: Know Yourself

1. Mary K. Dozier et al., "Attachment for Infants in Foster Care: The Role of Caregiver State of Mind," *Child Development* 72, no. 5 (2001): 1467–77; Howard Steele, Miriam Steele, and Peter Fonagy, "Associations Among Attachment Classifications of Mothers, Fathers, and Their Infants," *Child Development* 67 (1996): 541–55.

2. Selma Fraiberg, Edna Adelson, and Vivian Shapiro, "Ghosts in the Nursery: A Psychoanalytic Approach to the Problems of Impaired Infant-Mother Relationships," *Journal of the American Academy of Child Psychiatry* 14, no. 3 (1975): 387–421.

3. Jude Cassidy, "Truth, Lies, and Intimacy: An Attachment Perspective," *Attachment and Human Development* 3, no. 2 (2001): 121–55.

Chapter 3: Simplify with Scripts

1. Tiffany Field, Miguel Diego, and Maria Hernandez-Reif, "Prenatal Maternal Biochemistry Predicts Neonatal Biochemistry," *International Journal of Neuroscience* 11, no. 8 (2004): 933–45.

2. Theraplay is a child and family therapy for building and enhancing attachment, self-esteem, trust in others, and joyful engagement. With their permission, we have incorporated Theraplay strategies into our TBRI nurture groups, and we include their three rules—stick together, no hurts, and have fun—in our camps and trainings.

3. Mona D. Fishbane, "Wired to Connect: Neuroscience, Relationships, and Therapy," *Family Process* 46, no. 3 (2007): 395–412; Bessel A. Van der Kolk, "The Neurobiology of Childhood Trauma and Abuse," *Child and Adolescent Psychiatric Clinics of North America* 12 (2003): 293–317; Karyn B. Purvis et al., "A Spontaneous Emergence of Attachment Behavior in At-Risk Children and a Correlation with Sensory Deficits," *Journal of Child and Adolescent Psychiatric Nursing* 26 (2013): 165–72.

Chapter 4: Combat Chronic Fear

1. John Bowlby, *A Secure Base*, 2nd ed. (New York: Basic Books, 1988).

2. Megan R. Gunnar et al., "Salivary Cortisol Levels in Children Adopted from Romanian Orphanages," *Development and Psychopathology* 13, no. 3 (2001): 611–28.

3. Barbara Ganzel et al., "The Aftermath of 9/11: Effect of Intensity and Recency of Trauma on Outcome and Emotion," *Emotion* 7, no. 2 (2007): 227–38.

4. Paula Thompson, "'Down Will Come Baby': Prenatal Stress, Primitive Defenses and Gestational Dysregulation," *Journal of Trauma and Dissociation* 8, no. 3 (2007): 85–113.

5. Field, Diego, and Hernandez-Reif, "Prenatal Maternal Biochemistry," 933–45.

6. Karyn B. Purvis and David R. Cross, "Improvements in Salivary Cortisol, Depression, and Representations of Family Relationships in At-Risk Adopted Children Utilizing a Short-Term Therapeutic Intervention," *Adoption Quarterly* 10, no. 1 (2006): 25–43.

7. Purvis and Cross, "Improvements," 25–43.

Chapter 5: Nurture to Heal

1. Karyn B. Purvis, David R. Cross, and Wendy Lyons Sunshine, *The Connected Child: Bring Hope and Healing to Your Adoptive Family* (New York: McGraw-Hill, 2007), 145.

2. Cassidy, "Truth, Lies, and Intimacy," 121–55.

Chapter 6: Teach Respect

1. Purvis, Cross, and Sunshine, *The Connected Child*, 112.

2. Becker-Weidman, "Effects of Early Maltreatment on Development," 137–61.

3. Fishbane, "Wired to Connect," 395–412; Van der Kolk, "Neurobiology of Childhood Trauma," 293–317.

Chapter 7: Recognize Your Child's Sensory Needs

1. Roianne R. Ahn et al., "Prevalence of Parents' Perceptions of Sensory Processing Disorders Among Kindergarten Children," *American Journal of Occupational Therapy* 58 (2004): 287–93.

2. Purvis et al., "Spontaneous Emergence of Attachment Behavior," 165–72.

3. Tina Champagne, "The Influence of Posttraumatic Stress Disorder, Depression, and Sensory Processing Patterns on Occupational Engagement," *Journal of Prevention, Assessment, and Rehabilitation* 38, no. 1 (2011): 67–75; Kathleen S. Cummings, Sylvia A. Grandfield, and Craig M. Coldwell, "Caring with Comfort Rooms: Reducing Seclusion and Restraint Use in Psychiatric Facilities," *Journal of Psychosocial Nursing* 48 no. 6 (2010): 26–30; Brian Mullen, "Exploring the Safety and Therapeutic Effects of Deep Pressure Stimulation Using a Weighted Blanket," *Journal of Occupational Therapy in Mental Health* 24, no. 1 (2008): 65–89; Theresa Novak et al., "Pilot Study of a Sensory Room in an Acute Inpatient Psychiatric Unit," *Australasian Psychiatry* 20, no. 5 (2012): 401–6.

Chapter 9: Build Your Toolbox

1. Purvis, Cross, and Sunshine, *The Connected Child*, 98.

Chapter 10: Take Care of Yourself

1. National Child Traumatic Stress Network, Secondary Traumatic Stress Committee, *Secondary Traumatic Stress: A Fact Sheet for Child-Serving Professionals* (Los Angeles, CA: National Center for Child Traumatic Stress, 2011), https://www.nctsn.org/sites/default/files/resources/fact-sheet/secondary_traumatic_stress_child_serving_professionals.pdf.

2. Cited in a Powerpoint presentation by Dr. Purvis.

More Great Harvest House Books for Adoptive and Foster Parents

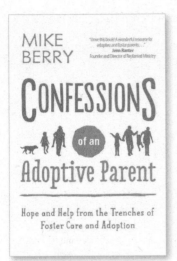

Confessions of an Adoptive Parent

Mike Berry

You Are Not Alone on This Journey

Adopting or fostering a child brings its own unique set of challenges only another parent facing the same uphill climb could possibly understand. From parenting children with traumatic pasts, to dealing with attachment issues, to raising a child with special needs, it can sometimes be a struggle just getting through the day.

Mike Berry knows the loneliness and isolation you can easily feel in your unique parenting role—because he's been there. He's *still there*, and he wants to give you the hope and encouragement you so desperately need.

There are plenty of how-to guides out there on parenting, but this one-of-a-kind book is specifically designed to address your needs as a parent of an adoptive or foster child. With a refreshing dose of honesty, empathy, and care, you'll discover that you are not alone on your journey and that God has a very special plan for you and your family.

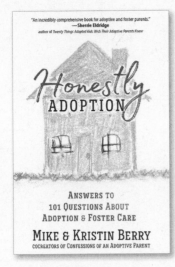

Honestly Adoption

Mike and Kristin Berry

Discover What Adoption and Foster Care Really Look Like

If you are considering adoption or foster care or are already somewhere in this difficult and complicated process, you need trusted information from people who have been where you are.

Mike and Kristin Berry have adopted eight children and cared for another twenty-three kids in their nine-year stint as foster parents. They aren't just experts; they have experienced every emotional high and low and encountered virtually every situation imaginable as parents. Now they want to share what they've learned with you.

Get the answers you need to the following questions and many more:

- Should I foster parent or adopt? How do I know?
- What is the first step in becoming an adoptive or foster parent?
- What are the benefits of an open versus closed adoption?
- How and when do I tell my child that he or she is adopted?
- How do I help my child embrace his or her cultural and racial identity?

Honestly Adoption will provide you with practical, down-to-earth advice on making good decisions in your own adoption and foster parenting journey and will give you the help and hope you need.

To learn more about Harvest House books and
to read sample chapters, visit our website:

www.harvesthousepublishers.com

HARVEST HOUSE PUBLISHERS
EUGENE, OREGON